HOPELESS BUT OPTIMISTIC

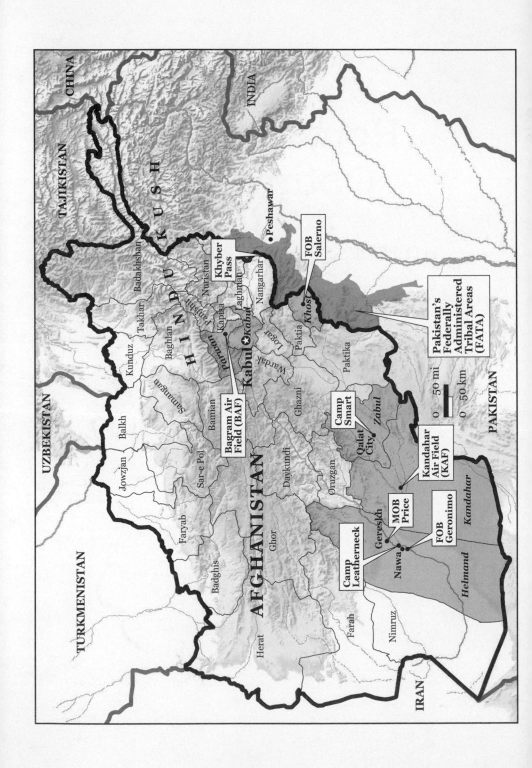

Hopeless but Optimistic

JOURNEYING THROUGH AMERICA'S ENDLESS WAR IN AFGHANISTAN

Douglas A. Wissing

INDIANA UNIVERSITY PRESS   *Bloomington & Indianapolis*

This book is a publication of

INDIANA UNIVERSITY PRESS
Office of Scholarly Publishing
Herman B Wells Library 350
1320 East 10th Street
Bloomington, Indiana 47405 USA

iupress.indiana.edu

The paper used in this publication meets
the minimum requirements of the
American National Standard for
Information Sciences—Permanence of
Paper for Printed Library Materials,
ANSI Z39.48-1992.

Manufactured in the United States of
America

Cataloging information is available from
the Library of Congress.

ISBN 978-0-253-02285-1 (cloth)
ISBN 978-0-253-02333-9 (ebook)

1 2 3 4 5   21 20 19 18 17 16

To my sons, Dylan and Seth

In any war story, but especially a true one, it's difficult to separate what happened from what seemed to happen. What seems to happen becomes its own happening and has to be told that way. The angles of vision are skewed.
—Tim O'Brien, *The Things They Carried*

Contents

List of Abbreviations

ACKU	Afghanistan Center at Kabul University
ADP-S	Alternative Development Program/Southern Region
ADT	agribusiness development team
ANA	Afghan National Army
ANAM	Automated Neuropsychological Assessment Metrics
ANSF	Afghan National Security Forces
AO [A/O]	area of operations
AP	Associated Press
ARD	Association for Rural Development
ASAP	Accelerating Sustainable Agriculture Program
ATFC	Afghan Threat Finance Cell
AVIPA	Afghanistan Vouchers for Increased Production in Agriculture
BAF	Bagram Air Field
BBC	British Broadcasting Corporation
BBIED	bicycle-borne improvised explosive device
B-hut	barracks hut
CCATT	Critical Care Air Transport Team
CCD	Community Center for the Disabled (mine victim support)
CERP	Commander's Emergency Response Program
CHAMP	Commercial Horticulture and Agricultural Marketing Program (USAID)
CIA	Central Intelligence Agency
COIN	counterinsurgency
COR	contracting officer's representative
CRCC	Concussion Restoration Care Center
C-SIG	cross-cutting, senior-level group
DAIL	Director of Agriculture, Irrigation, and Livestock
DATC	District Agricultural Training Center
DCA	Dutch Committee for Afghanistan
DFAC	dining facility
DRMO	Defense Reutilization and Marketing Office
ECP	entry control point
EOD	explosive ordnance detection

FOB   forward operating base
FUD   female urinary device
GAO   Government Accountability Office
GDP   gross domestic product
GIROA   Government of the Islamic Republic of Afghanistan
HAVA   Helmand-Arghandab Valley Authority
IBA   individual body armor
IED   improvised explosive device
IESCO   Islamic Educational, Scientific, and Cultural Organization
IO   information operations
IRD   International Relief and Development
ISAF   International Security Assistance Force
JIEDDO   Joint Improvised Explosive Device Defeat Organization
JPEL   Joint Prioritized Effects List
KAF   Kandahar Air Field
KIA   Kabul International Airport; killed in action
LZ   landing zone
MAIL   Ministry of Agriculture, Irrigation, and Livestock
MANPADS   man-portable air-defense system
MOB   main operating base
MRAP   mine-resistant ambush protected
MRE   meal, ready to eat
NATO   North Atlantic Treaty Organization
NDS   National Directorate of Security
NGO   nongovernmental organization
PA   public affairs
PAO   public affairs officer
PAX   passenger air terminal
PB   patrol base
PRT   provincial reconstruction team
PTSD   post-traumatic stress disorder
PX   post exchange
QA/QC   quality assurance/quality controlled
QIP   quick-impact projects
RAMP   Rebuilding Agricultural Markets Program
R&R   rest and recuperation
RCP   Route Clearance Package
RPG   rocket-propelled grenade
SAS   Special Air Service
SIGAR   Special Inspector General for Afghanistan Reconstruction
SOCOM   Special Operations Command
TBI   traumatic brain injury
TICS   troops in combat
UN   United Nations
USAID   United States Agency for International Development
USDA   United States Department of Agriculture
VFU   Veterinary Field Unit (DCA)

WHAM	winning hearts and minds
WIT	Women in Transition
WPA	Works Progress Administration (New Deal); War Projects Administration (Afghanistan War)

HOPELESS BUT OPTIMISTIC

Prologue

IN EARLY 2013 I EMBEDDED FOR THE THIRD TIME WITH US troops in insurgency-racked Afghanistan. A Midwestern grandfather with a bad back, I humped a hundred pounds of gear across the Afghan war zones searching for the ground truth as US officials cynically spun a victory narrative, American soldiers tried to keep their body parts together, and Afghans strained to figure out their next move. This book is an impressionistic close-up of America's interminable war in Afghanistan.

While this book is about America's post-9/11 war in Afghanistan, it is also about eternal war. Why humans go to war, how they learn to love and hate, how they keep it together when it's clearly going wrong, the prices they pay. It's also about why and how journalists follow the battles. It's about that deep curiosity to understand humans in extremis, both others and ourselves.

Hopeless but Optimistic: Journeying through America's Endless War in Afghanistan is also about the US government's twenty-first-century way of waging war. The American government has never privatized a war to this extent, and it has given rise to horrific dysfunction that has cost Americans a trillion dollars while failing to accomplish its military and diplomatic goals. I detailed the story of the failed counterinsurgency with thousands of citations in my *Funding the Enemy: How US Taxpayers Bankroll the Taliban* (Prometheus Books, 2012). This work is not volume two of that book. This is a narrative about my quest to see if American officials and officers had learned any lessons from their failures. The

1

import is clear: the selfsame interest groups want to take the same failed strategy to other chaotic battlefields in the Middle East and Africa.

⠇   ⠇   ⠇   ⠇   ⠇

The Afghanistan War is not unique. Former diplomat Peter Van Buren's scathing critique of the Iraq counterinsurgency, *We Meant Well*, unveiled the same failed policies in another post-9/11 conflict. Thomas Ricks's and Andrew Bacevich's critical analyses depicted an ever more ineffective American military culture. The research and writings of foreign aid critics Dambisa Moyo, William Easterly, and Nobel Prize–winning economist Angus Deaton revealed the West's self-serving "phantom aid" to the underdeveloped world. Through these and other thinkers, I began to understand the Afghanistan War as part of a systemic problem.

Political thinker Mike Lofgren's provocative essay "Anatomy of the Deep State" gave me a framework to think about the powers that undergird the American political system. In Lofgren's matrix, the Deep State is a hybrid of the government's national security and law enforcement agencies, the increasingly powerful private military, intelligence and development corporations, and Wall Street and Silicon Valley, which have all benefited so mightily from incessant privatized war.

Americans are understanding that the Deep State's hierarchy is failing to accomplish their stated goals, and in the process is not serving broader societal needs. So this book is also a case study of the declining American empire, its imperial delusions and self-aggrandizing ways. As I journeyed across Afghanistan, where over millennia so many empires have come to bad ends, I began to see the country as the graveyard of America's Deep State.

And this is about the Afghans, those resilient people who taught me so much. One gray day in Kabul toward the end of my journey across embattled Afghanistan, I interviewed a suave government official in his gloomy office, which overlooked an Afghan kindergarten that the CIA had inexplicably built. In some ways, his life embodied Afghanistan's turbulent recent history. His family had fled the 1980s US-supported ghost war that pitted the mujahideen against the Soviet-backed Afghan government. They stayed away during Afghanistan's cataclysmic civil war after the jihadis defeated the Soviets and the United States withdrew. Educated in exile, he returned to Afghanistan in the post-9/11 surge of American money and troops that brought so many expatriate Afghans back. He witnessed the explosion of corruption and violence that followed. Sitting dapper in his government sinecure in the twilight of another American withdrawal, the perky technocrat, ever the survivor, was weighing his options. When I asked him about the future for Afghans, he looked me in the eye and confidently said, "I am hopeless—but optimistic." Another government minister wryly told me, "We are optimistic. We're Afghans. What else can we be?" Like the Afghans, I am hopeless, but optimistic.

ONE

Landing

KABUL INTERNATIONAL AIRPORT: INCOMING SOLDIERS LIKE to chuckle at Kabul's airport code, KIA—"killed in action." My Safi Airways flight from Dubai descends at dawn, and the light tints the snowcapped mountains that picket Kabul orange, then pink, then a deep rose. Across the aisle, a muscular American in khaki tactical clothes stares straight ahead, deep in thought, face half in shadow, the sunlight reflecting in his eyes as the plane banks over the adobe-brown city with its yellow dome of pollution.

As we approach landing, I have my own reasons for pensiveness. Beyond the standard war trepidation, I'm uneasy about my approvals to embed with US troops. This is my third trip to cover the Afghanistan War, but getting US military approvals has been far more problematic this time, perhaps because my book *Funding the Enemy* had revealed the US counterinsurgency's systemic dysfunction. Didn't make me any friends in the Pentagon, an intelligence guy told me. So when military PAOs (public affairs officers) repeatedly canceled my approvals for embeds in the volatile eastern and southern battle spaces, I wasn't surprised. One PAO sent a testy e-mail asking if I wrote "The Juice Ain't Worth the Squeeze," a critical *Foreign Policy* article. Seemed an odd question, given that my name was right under the title. Another canceled embed. It was only after I announced I was flying to Kabul to arrange things from there that the embed approvals seem to come back and firm up—maybe. I didn't know what to expect.

Why am I so intent on going back? I'm afflicted with the writer's delirium: I want to know how the story ends. After all the scandals, the whistleblowers, the critical media and books, the revelations by an array of inspectors general, the scathing congressional investigations, I want to see if the system has reformed. As America's endgame in Afghanistan plays out, have there been any lessons learned, or are the same malign networks that connected ambitious American careerists, greedy US corporations, corrupt Afghan kleptocrats, and the Taliban still pulsing with wasted American tax dollars? As I descend into Kabul a dozen years after the war started, the US government is still pouring $1.5 billion a *week* into Afghanistan. Sixty-eight thousand American soldiers and probably twice that many contractors are ostensibly (and futilely) trying to bind Afghans to the predatory Karzai government. The Taliban controls major parts of the country. Given these bleak facts, what is the mood of the troops, the contractors, the aid workers, the diplomats, the Afghans? What's going to happen to Afghanistan? I want to know.

But as the plane dips toward the runway, I am more concerned with the fifty-kilometer taxi ride from KIA to BAF (Bagram Air Field), where I am to report for embeds. Just going through Kabul is considered a risky proposition, and the road between KIA and BAF stretches across the dangerous Shomali Plain. Because of the security problem, virtually all Westerners—military, diplomats, contractors, and journalists—now fly the short distance to BAF on small military planes from the military side of the Kabul airport. In my previous embed, the military had arranged for me to fly into BAF almost as a matter of course. But not this time. "Take a taxi," the PAO e-mailed. I'd done it in 2009, using a trusted Afghan taxi service, so that's my plan.

Back in the glitzy Dubai International Airport, the Kabul-bound passengers had buddied up in an almost reflexive way. A group of expat Afghan women returning for family reunions bonded over how to wear their unfamiliar headscarves in Kabul. "Maybe it is our last chance to go, with the Americans . . . leaving," a Tajik woman from Fremont said quietly. A fleshy Skol-spitting contractor sauntered over and sat down beside me. He monitored rocket attacks at FOB (forward operating base) Sharana, a bleak logistic base that I'd been to. He said security wasn't too bad at Sharana, but was deteriorating as US troops increasingly stayed in their compounds. "Small FOBs getting hit all the time—no patrols," he said. "Getting closer all the time." When he heard about my plan to taxi to Bagram, his eyes widened. "No way," he said. A bulky black man with a baby face joined us. Kind eyes, a quick, solid grace. Said he'd been a special forces sergeant, but now was a shooter for one of those Blackwater-cloned private security contractors that thronged Afghanistan. Worked out of a fortified company compound in Kabul. "Triple the money and half the oversight," he said. When the attendants called our flight, a solitary young Afghan woman with frightened eyes lined up beside us. In a lilting British accent she said she hadn't been back to Afghanistan for sixteen years. "I feel safer being with Western people," she said nervously as she tucked a wisp of hair into her headscarf. I asked if someone was meeting her in Kabul. "Oh yes," she said with a broad smile of relief. "My uncle."

After our plane lands at Kabul International Airport, we file down the aluminum stairway to the waiting buses. The KIA terminal is a Brutalist concrete expression of international solidarity that looks downright Stalinist, which makes sense given that the Soviets built the airfield and terminal during the Cold War. We are a glum, sober group. The informal partners reunite. I see the Tajik women have adopted the young returnee. She helps them adjust their headscarves as we head for the terminal. We abruptly arrive in scarcely ordered Afghanistan. Milling and grabbing porters, officious factotums, sullen security guards with automatic weapons. I scramble for my bags, that awful hundred pounds of body armor, Kevlar, computer, cameras, clothes, recorders, files, notebooks, and survival gadgets: penlight with red lens for blacked-out combat bases, Swiss Army knife, an odd little solar charger, duct tape, safety pins, first aid kit, and a plastic ziplock bag with about a pound of lucky charms given to me by loved ones.

The porters descend on the travelers waiting for their luggage. The Sharana contractor's porter quickly wheels off his large, hard-shelled tool case, which is the preferred luggage for war-zone commuters. The contractor nods to me as he follows his porter down the hall. The black shooter comes over while a small, wizened Afghan is wrestling my bags onto a rickety cart. "My peeps are coming to pick me up," he says. "I'm right in Kabul. That fifteen minutes is the most dangerous part of this job. Ooow, you're an hour out there . . ." He walks away shaking his head.

: : : : :

I'd been warned countless times that kidnapping is a cottage industry in Afghanistan. Don't get into unfamiliar taxis. So my trusted taxi driver needs to be there. I worry as I leave the security cordon surrounding the main terminal and shoulder my way through the crowds of Afghans waiting near the parking lot. I nervously call the cell number the taxi company has given me. A crisp voice answers: "This is Nawab." He tells me where to find him in the parking lot. He'll be looking for me. And as I come out the door, there he is.

Nawab is a slender, smiling Tajik in a gray polyester double-breasted jacket and a plaid shirt. He waves as I walk toward him and opens the trunk to help with my bags. The final security checkpoints and we are in the thrum of war-fueled Kabul.

It's cold and murky. The smell of petrol, maybe brimstone. Herds of fat-tailed sheep and donkeys pulling tiny carts share the road with racing Corollas, pickups, motorcycles, and armored SUVs. It's wild, anarchic traffic—vehicular Russian roulette. Laborers stomp down the road. Women in faded blue burqas squat at the verge. There are Afghan police and soldiers everywhere, along with evidence of the failed counterinsurgency. Faded anti-Taliban posters that just seem sad and futile. CCD (Community Center for the Disabled) trucks with red "Danger!" signs graphically advertising Afghanistan's land-mine peril and the tens of thousands of victims. A USAID (United States Agency for International Development) billboard proclaiming women's rights in English and Dari that few Afghan females can read, because almost 90 percent of them are still illiterate after more than a decade and $100 billion spent on grotesquely mismanaged US aid programs. The quagmire, we are in it. "Pouring money in the sand pit," soldiers repeatedly told me. The great, dollar-sucking sand pile of Afghanistan. The Taliban dictum has long been "The Americans have the watches, but we have the time." And time is running out for the Americans.

As we drive through the city, I can see both boomtown Kabul and Kabul in bust. There's the Kabubble, with its sleek office towers and garish multistory wedding halls—City Star, Qasre Uranus, Afghan Kyber.

Nawab points to French-themed Sham e Paris with its light-bedecked mock Eiffel Tower. "It is Las Vegas—yes?" Then there is the bust: the paved roads that suddenly give way to rubble; half-finished construction projects shrouded in plastic tarps like rectangular corpses; cur dogs scrapping in the mountainous garbage piles. Looming over a ramshackle stall with a tarp roof, a hand-painted sign proclaims, "New Ci-tee Dairy Superstore." The Kabul New City development—another of the megalomaniac wet dreams that captured the US and Afghan insiders' imagination in the postinvasion boom days of unlimited international development money. Officially it was Dehsabz City, but flacks called it Skyscraper City. Envisioned as an immense megadevelopment stretching out into the Shomali Plain with half a million housing units, industrial parks, agribusinesses, nature parks, and so on, it was to be mostly financed with billions of dollars of international development aid. Lots of money to be made with landgrabs and graft and bloated consultant contracts. Hard-ons galore in board rooms and government offices.

But like the Dairy Superstore shack, the New City is turning out to be a fantasy. The New City is, of course, another wholly inappropriate development for Afghanistan, a basket case of a country with a per capita GDP of about $400. The country sits at the bottom of virtually every development index, from life expectancy to electricity. About 97 percent of Afghanistan's licit gross domestic product comes from international military and development aid. The real economy's main exports are opium and heroin. It is a violent warrior culture riven with centuries-old tribal enmities. The Government of the Islamic Republic of Afghanistan, GIROA in the military parlance, is thoroughly and systemically corrupt. This is a failed state, not the Las Vegas of central Asia.

As we motor toward the Shomali Plain, I ask Nawab about how things look to him. "Day by day, it's better," he says, almost by rote. "But the foreigners are going," and he shrugs.

TWO

Problems

LONG AFTER AMERICA INVADED AFGHANISTAN, THE SHOMALI Plain is still a treacherous place, one of the world's most active land-mine areas. But at least the way to Bagram is easier than my journey in 2009, when my taxi driver had to slowly weave across the bomb-cratered plain, following braided dirt tracks to the air base. Back then soldiers regaled me with tales of wild, high-speed rides to Kabul, dodging snipers, decades-old mines, and fresh IEDs (improvised explosive devices). The new Kabul–Bagram highway opened in 2010, courtesy of the Army Corps of Engineers and US taxpayers. Albeit another absurdly expensive US-built road, it seems almost worth it as we grandly course along the comforting carapace of black asphalt toward the snow-dusted mountains and BAF's promised security.

The morning is bright and sunny, the five-thousand-foot-high air crisp and clear. Nawab dials the radio and the percussive beat and shrill notes of Afghan pop music leaches out of the speakers. Large villages and tilled fields stretching into the distance speak of Shomali's agricultural importance. Along the way, abandoned construction sites, tattered billboards, and roads leading off to chimeric New City developments stand beside the highway. When I ask Nawab about the apparent lack of progress on the megacity, he smiles and says things have slowed down since the Americans announced their withdrawal.

Following the public affairs officer's directive, I phone as we progress toward Bagram Air Field, the United States' largest base in Afghanistan. "About a half hour out," I report, handing the phone to Nawab so he can confirm our destination. "Call back when you're ten minutes out," the sergeant tells me when Nawab returns the phone. We are heading to ECP 3 (Entry Control Point 3), the main vehicle entrance. Been there before and knew the journalist pick-up drill. When I arrived in my little white taxi in 2009, there was a momentary wait before the massive steel gate rumbled open and an armored gun truck with army publicists in full battle rattle rolled out to fetch me and my stuff. In a flash, we were in the womb of Mother BAF.

Bagram Air Field is the largest US base in Afghanistan. Impounded behind more than eleven miles of meandering security walls and razor wire, the base's five thousand acres are crammed with the air field, command headquarters, office buildings, hospitals, spec ops facilities, roads, housing, rec centers, gyms, classrooms, and a strip mall. With thousands of soldiers and fleets of aircraft and vehicles, BAF is a big, fat target for Taliban rocket and mortar attacks launched from the neighboring villages. In a tense meeting in one of those villages a few years before, a gimlet-eyed security soldier from Kentucky had drawled to me, "It didn't work out so well for the Russians here." While the village leaders enthusiastically feigned US allegiance for promised development money, Taliban fighters imperiously watched from a nearby bluff. The soldier glanced up and said, "It ain't workin' out so good for *us*. These *pee-pul* don't like *anybody*."

The gate at ECP 3 is particularly dangerous. When Vice President Dick Cheney was on BAF in 2007, a Taliban suicide bomber detonated his vehicle bomb in ECP 3, killing twenty-three and wounding twenty. When Cheney finally emerged from a bomb shelter, he told reporters the audacious attacks "shouldn't affect our behavior at all." In some ways it didn't. Soldiers complained that BAF force protection was a joke, with high vegetation along the perimeter fences and housing built close to the walls. The sandbags and reinforced concrete of 2005 gave way to thousands of frail plywood B-huts (barracks huts).

In the spring of 2010, the Taliban began to probe Bagram's defenses, including with a rocket attack that killed a contractor in a B-hut. In May 2010, insurgents wearing suicide vests and US Army uniforms attacked BAF. A dozen heavily armed insurgents rushed ECP 1, the pedestrian gate in the Bagram town bazaar. But that was a feint. The real focus was just north of ECP 3—a brazen, full-frontal assault on the largest base in Afghanistan. Equipped with IEDs, RPGs (rocket-propelled grenades), and AK-47s, the Taliban fighters penetrated the perimeter fence, took a guard tower after the Afghan soldiers fled, and began hurling grenades at the nearby housing. It was an eight-hour firefight with ten US casualties.

So ECP 3 is definitely not a place I want to linger. As we turn onto the dirt road leading to the gate, we pass a new concrete bazaar that Nawab says is owned by a high-ranking Afghan official. I call the public affairs sergeant. We are getting close. Rooster tails of dust billow behind us as we jounce into the rutted truck yard of ECP 3. The high concrete walls of Bagram Air Field loom ahead. An Afghan soldier waves us to a stop at a concrete emplacement, where a clutch of disheveled security guards lounge in resigned torpor. Glancing in the taxi, he waves us on. I call again, say we are in front of the gate. And then it gets hairy. The PAOs can't or won't let me on the base. Sergeant says they have to get my paperwork. Have to wake up the officer. Have to get a truck. They need time. Need to wait.

It's a shock to be marooned outside the gate; stomach-tightening. ECP 3 is BAF's "soak yard," the muddy, rocky field where hundreds of tankers and supply trucks from central and south Asia wait for a day before being allowed inside the base's tall walls. The operant theory is that the twenty-four-hour wait allows for hidden explosives to soak through their wrappings so the K-9 bomb dogs can sniff them out. Sometimes the trucks just blow up. The yard has a simmering menace, like a medieval encampment below a besieged battlement. Hard-faced drivers begin to eye us. Nawab turns off the radio, places his hands on the wheel, and stares straight ahead.

It's a circumscribed, prison-block view: parallax concrete and patch of sky. The wall stretches into the distance, with watchtowers studding the sides. A tethered white surveillance dirigible levitates overhead. Communication and aviation control towers spike the skyline. The yellow-tinged air is heavy with the stench of aviation fuel. Fighter planes scream into the murk with a roar of afterburner. Chinooks churn off on their errands of supply and death. The mountains beyond BAF are hazy, indistinct.

As time creeps by, I begin to realize the PAOs aren't going to whisk me into BAF. Something else is going on. Nawab begins to deconstruct the scene around us. Hundreds of trucks are parked in a vaguely ordered jumble. He points out a deep-orange truck that has traveled the embattled road from Kandahar, laughing as he says "So dangerous," as though the achievement is more crazy than courageous. There are dozens of trucks from Pakistan, from Turkmenistan, from Mazar-e-Sharif. The intricately painted Afghan and Pakistani jingle trucks tinkle and rattle as the wind riffles the hanging chains and chimes. Gargantuan gravel trucks piled high with broken rock roar into the yard belching black diesel smoke. I watch wistfully as Afghan soldiers wave them through the outer checkpoint, and then on through the BAF gate with scarcely a tap on their air brakes. Clearly a lot of construction still going on.

Nawab points to a festooned black tanker. "From Herat. Petrol. From Iran." And he shakes his head. "Another," he says, nodding toward another tanker. Politically connected smugglers truck embargoed Iranian oil across the border into western Afghanistan, where it joins the great river of oil pouring into America's fuel-sucking war. With oil imported through Pakistan and down the northern routes costing the Pentagon up to $600 a gallon for "in-theater delivery" to soldiers in the field, and Iranian oil costing a pittance, there is big money to be made. And that is what the war in Afghanistan is all about.

The waiting drivers are a human inventory of central and south Asia: A tall bearded Pashtun with a black turban and stately carriage. Quick-stepping little Pakistanis, who move in schools. A Hazara with a wispy beard who could have rode with Genghis Khan. A burly Uzbek in a thick coat. A slender Baloch from the west. Caucasian faces with green eyes that tell of Alexander the Great's Grecian forays. As the sun warms the yard, an exuberance of peddlers begin to flock. Alert young boys in flapping rubber boots push old wheelbarrows filled with soft drinks, water, and snacks. A small Afghan manhandles the tiny wheels of his small blue-painted food stand across the lot's fist-sized rocks. A second, better-nourished vendor follows soon after, positioning his larger, canopied food stand beside the first. Both lay out stacks of flatbread naan. The smells of lamb kabobs and *bendee*, the classic Afghan turmeric-tinged okra, tomatoes, and onions, begin to waft across the field, gathering a cluster of drivers. I get out, thinking I'll wander over. Heads swivel. Nawab sits wide-eyed, eyebrows up. Hands back on the wheel. I get back in.

Another hour passes. Afghan men begin to stride purposefully by the taxi, slowing to peer at the American outlier. An old woman suddenly appears at the window, startling me. Tapping the window, tapping, her ancient hand moving to her mouth, moving to her mouth, tapping, tapping. Nawab shakes his head. A woman shrouded in a faded blue burqa holds her young son's hand as she methodically begs across the field, stopping at cars, then trucks, then the crowd of drivers. A man with a flat wool *pakol* cap maneuvers his crutches across the field, his twisted legs dangling beneath him.

The Afghan "truck lord" occasionally wanders through with his clipboard and trailing assistant. The drivers gather to await his decisions regarding their BAF entry, which are, of course, connected to the size of their contributions to his "retirement fund." An Apache helicopter rears up from the base and speeds north; an F-16 with its nose arrogantly lifted swoops down for a landing. The black steel gates whoosh open and a small convoy of armored MRAPS (mine-resistant ambush-protected vehicles) rushes out as a red-and-white crossbar drops behind them. My PAO pickup at last? The convoy races down the road to Kabul.

Then the cell phone rings. The PAO: "Procedures changed. Maybe you should drive back to Kabul and fly into BAF." My heart sinks. Maybe this is all a ruse to get me to retreat back to Kabul. Maybe they will never let me on a military plane out of Kabul. I am ready to object when there is a pause; a muffled conference, and then: "Maybe you should wait. A PAO lost her escort badge. Security's demanding she fill out new paperwork and come back for the badge at 11:00. But they're at lunch now." This is just plain scary. I remember being in a bazaar in insurgency-plagued Khost Province, where the security soldiers insisted the team only had fourteen minutes to accomplish their development mission before the insurgents could dispatch a suicide bomber. Is this a useful recollection at this moment? Hours have gone by, and I am still a live sitting duck—a very nervous, live sitting duck. But I wait.

Another hour and a half before the phone rings again. "We have another problem," the sergeant quickly says. "Changed procedures." The air force gatekeepers now refuse to let any "pedestrians" come in through ECP 3, though I am an American citizen to be picked up in an American truck and driven onto the base by American soldiers. The PAO says I have to drive around the base and enter though the bazaar entrance, ECP 1. Out of control outside the walls; an epidemic of OCD inside. I tell Nawab what the PAO said. He looks surprised. "ECP 1? In the bazaar?" I ask if he knows where it is. "I know," he says, and starts the taxi.

THREE

In/Out

BAGRAM'S SEEN PLENTY OF AMBITIOUS, CULTURALLY HYPHEN-
ated empires. The Persians under Cyrus the Great conquered Bagram
about 2,500 years ago. A few centuries later Alexander the Great established his fortified Greek colony of Alexandria of the Caucasus at
Bagram. The Indian Mauryans followed. So did the Sunga, the Greco-
Bactrians, the Indo-Greek Eucratidians, the Yuezki, the Kushans.
Britain's Anglo-Indian empire surged through the region in the nineteenth century. The Soviet empire made Bagram Air Field an important
redoubt during the Afghan-Communist era. Of course, they all fell.
Somewhere in the ancient city of Bagram, a turbaned antiquarian must
have been cackling at the current American-Afghan folly.

Nawab wheels us out of the soak yard toward ECP 1, the pedestrian
gate about five miles away in the middle of Bagram's town bazaar. Jericho
flashes through my mind as we speed past BAF's towering walls. Thousands of Afghans enter ECP 1 daily to do the base's scut work—washing
laundry, cleaning latrines, digging ditches, selling handcrafts at BAF's
haji shops—but Nawab only has a rough idea where ECP 1 is located, as
I am his first international passenger to have to use it. So when we arrive
we have to make a nerve-racking reconnoiter through the crowded bazaar, first by taxi and then by foot, lugging my gear through the warren
of rough wooden stands selling oranges and apples and long white radishes. Posters of Afghan pop singers and the slain mujahideen Massoud
hang above piles of gewgaws, cheap electronics, and CDs. Butted up
against the BAF walls, it is neo-tribal central Asia spooning with Little

America. Seems like the perfect place for insurgents to insinuate themselves.

We are looking for the Russian Gate, the fortified entry point to the one-thousand-yard-long security gauntlet the Afghan workers traverse each day. An Afghan trader eventually directs us to the reinforced concrete emplacement that is almost hidden among the stalls. I finally make it into BAF—but no. Scowling Afghan private security guards stop me from entering, waving me back, barring the way, demanding I wait in the bazaar until my American escorts arrive. By this time I am exhausted from twenty-four hours of travel, jet lag, and tension. My packs seem to be getting heavier. I worry Nawab is in danger. Just as I reach for my cell phone to see if I can get some American intercession, an Afghan higher-up tells the guards to let me wait inside the gate. They don't look happy, but I am. Nawab waves good-bye as he disappears back into the bazaar.

Two PAO sergeants arrive red-faced and fully armed, flustered and apologetic for the gate problems, huffing from their mile-long charge across BAF in their hundred pounds of IBAS (individual body armor) and gear. Changed procedures, they tell me. Increased security; turf battles between the services. Air force that handles gate security made an example out of me to punish the PA office. These things happen. Should have flown in from Kabul (though their boss, now on R&R, insisted I take the taxi). Relieved, angry, appreciative, tetchy, suspicious. I am cycling emotions at a rapid clip. Is it going to be this way for the rest of the trip?

The Afghan guards search my bags, tossing ransacked gear everywhere. Looks as though a small IED has gone off. Stuffing what I can back in my bags, I strap on my body armor and start to load up when one of the sergeants cheerfully offers to haul my packs. It's a no-no. Journalists are supposed to haul their own stuff. His buddy says to me, "Aw, let him do it. He's always trying to carry more weight." At this point, their simple human kindness almost unnerves me.

One sergeant suddenly asks about the Afghan vegetables piled in the bazaar just outside the gate. The bazaar is off limits to them. For 90 percent of the US soldiers in Afghanistan, "outside the wire" is alien territory. Says he envies me, wants to "cook some real food." He can have it. I am grateful to be inside the wire. Even with the sergeant carrying most of my gear, I am running on fumes.

As we negotiate the long security channel, I catch glimpses of the military's determined order and a thicket of construction cranes: the signifiers of Late Empire American energy. Exhausted or not, I am curious about the BAF construction. Is the frenetic building pace at Bagram continuing despite the withdrawal? I ask the PAOs about the gravel trucks I saw coming through ECP 3. With the scheduled drawdown of forces, what is the long-term plan for Bagram? Trudging along with my baggage, the sergeant says with a snort, "My long-term is four months." When I look at him, he says, "That's when we rotate out. I'm ready to go." His buddy agrees. "We're from Oregon; the unit's from Oregon. We're ready to go home."

FOUR

Reify

THE SERGEANT IS A CRUSTY VET WITH A GRAY BRUSH CUT and a wrinkled grandpa face. Peering over his rimless glasses, he looks like the geezer in a cowboy show. "They hit us on Christmas Day," he says, "and about three months ago three mortar shells hit the PAX [passenger air terminal], but two were duds." Speaking of Afghanistan's intelligence agency, the National Directorate of Security (NDS), he tells me, "There was the rocket attack a while back that destroyed a Chinook and killed some Afghan NDS guys. You ask probably any of these infantry guys, and they'll say let's get the fuck out of here. This is a fucked place. What the fuck are we doing here?"

As he drives me around Bagram, the place seems bipolar. For a dozen years military orders have alternated between "Don't build anything permanent; we're not going to be here long," and "We are going to be here a very long time, so build a fortress." So while there are still lots of troops and offices in ragged tents, metal shipping containers, and delaminating plywood B-huts, the massive $200 million construction project that began in 2009 is still in full swing, even as the troop withdrawal rapidly depletes the boots on the ground. Ah, government contracts. We drive past the multistory, hardened division headquarters built on the site of the old Soviet hanger (where Bagram lore has it that the mujahideen castrated and hung the last Russians). Along Disney Drive, BAF's main drag, Afghan laborers are busy digging a deep sewer line. The sergeant points out the new Warfighter Restoration Center and the giant special forces compound, uniquely equipped with indoor plumbing.

"Water inside. That's a big deal here," he said, grumbling about his quarter-mile hike to the lavatories.

Beyond their military effectiveness, the special forces soldiers also give poll-sensitive politicians an additional benefit: Since the spec ops teams are seldom rotated into Afghanistan for more than six months, they don't have to be counted as "boots on the ground." The American public need never know the true number of soldiers in Afghanistan. Sweet.

The sergeant is part of the post-9/11 wars' "Gray Brigade," older soldiers in reserve and National Guard units who have repeatedly been called up for duty. Lots of gray hair and wrinkles on big bases like Bagram, almost as though the military has an "aging in place" policy for the AARP crowd. As we pull into the parking lot, the sergeant unexpectedly says, "I'm hoping to come back." He volunteers that it isn't because of a love of Afghanistan or freedom-fighting for democracy or fighting the terrorists here rather than in New York. No, it's benefits. He's career military with three years to retirement. I ask if another deployment will sweeten his retirement. "Oh yes," he says with a foxy smile. "It's not so bad here."

∷   ∷   ∷   ∷   ∷

A light knock on the door wakes me out of a jet-lagged nap. Virtually every American journalist covering Afghanistan has to pass through BAF's Hotel California, the small brown plywood B-hut dorm that the Public Affairs Office maintains for transiting press. Barebones: bunk beds, wooden shelves for desks, wastebasket seats. Almost inevitably, a wall mural reads, "You can check out any time you like / But you can never leave." The young captain who knocked says the colonel in charge of public affairs wants to meet with me—dinner?

The DFACs (dining facilities) are hubs of military life in Afghanistan. Whether masonry structures constructed to withstand direct rocket hits or vulnerable inflatable tents, the DFACs reflect the soldiers' world. Beside the serried lines of brown Formica tables, signs read, "Do Not Place Weapons on Floor." Remarkable how quickly you get used to dining with hundreds of armed soldiers, each packing enough firepower to take out a shopping mall. After an obligatory hand scrub at the entry area, there are cafeteria lines with amazingly diverse foods, from steak, fried foods, taco bars, and junk food to salad bars and health food. Vegetables from Dubai (no Afghan produce—fear of poisoning), Texas Pete Original Hot Sauce, Uzbekistan fruit drink in Cyrillic-lettered boxes. Printed cards rate each dish as a low-, medium-, or high-performing food, nudging me toward chicken, rice, and salad.

I pass one table where soldiers are complaining about the military's plans to cut hot breakfasts. Fight the Taliban without bacon? Food is so plentiful, it creates problems for combat soldiers intent on keeping fit. At one frontline base, I saw graffiti scratched into a toilet stall wall. "I am going to die," it read. I naturally visualized a young soldier taking advantage of a little privacy to express his grave fears. It was only later that I realized the graffiti actually read, "I am going to diet."

Lurid florescent light gives the white windowless dining facilities a low-budget sci-fi look. A wall poster that depicts Superman with bowed head and clenched fists advertises combat stress control classes. Weekly groups on anger, stress, and time management, sleep hygiene and relaxation training at the Warfighter Restoration Center.

The colonel and his deputy are articulate; clearly facile in working with the media; witty in that droll war-zone way. Taut, trim, well educated, organizationally deft: twenty-first-century military leaders. Around us, there is the hum and murmur of a hundred conversations, the scraping of metal chairs on concrete, the clatter of weaponry, an occasional Velcro rip of body armor. Young soldiers with raging metabolisms arrive with pasteboard trays piled high with starches and fried things. Older officers walk past with sparse trays: a turkey wing and salad; the Oriental medley. Sullen Afghan men, their dark hair and beards bagged in white netting, bus the room. After pleasantries and preliminaries, the three of us begin talking about Generals David Petraeus and Stanley McChrystal, with whom both officers had worked. Though an effective commander, McChrystal was forced to resign in June 2010 after *Rolling Stone* published Michael Hastings's story about McChrystal's staff officers mocking civilian leaders, including President Barack Obama and Vice President Joe Biden—called "Bite-me" in one memorable quote. After McChrystal resigned, Petraeus commanded in Afghanistan until July

2011. Sworn in as CIA director in October 2011, Petraeus resigned a year later after an extramarital affair with his biographer Paula Broadwell became known. Broadwell's smarmy book title, *All In*, said it all. The colonel and his deputy began talking about the two generals' different operating styles: The colonel says, "McChrystal was about operations and Petraeus was about IO [information operations]." The deputy adds, "Virtually any issue, Petraeus would ask his staffers, 'How does this affect my IO? How does this affect my IO?'"

A master press manipulator, Petraeus used the media to trumpet his intellect, accomplishments, and counterinsurgency strategy—even while it was failing in Afghanistan. Petraeus's IO tactics were even more alarming because the military essentially merged information operations, with its imperative for propaganda and deception, with public affairs functions, which are intended to inform the American public and its elected representatives. It made a toxic cocktail of press relations and psychological warfare. It fueled an entrenched misinformation system that produced what Pentagon whistleblower Lieutenant Colonel Daniel Davis termed "the truth deficit" in Afghanistan. Davis charged General Petraeus with deceiving the American people with a "victory narrative" while the political and military situation in Afghanistan was actually cratering.

While Petraeus was commanding the war effort, I had spoken with an old Afghanistan hand working in the American embassy in Kabul. He told me US policy wonks in Kabul and Washington had a new buzzword: "reify." Ruefully laughing, he explained, "'Reify' refers to a concept being confused with reality. In the eleventh year of a failing war in Afghanistan, it's about as good a word as any to use to describe the US situation."

After witnessing Petraeus's disastrous counterinsurgency strategy, I couldn't fault Davis's analysis. It's obvious to me there is little correlation between the happy talk promulgated from podiums in Washington and the on-the-ground reality in Afghanistan. USAID "Success Stories" are more like tales of Potemkin villages. The State Department's calm assurances that all is fine are delusional, as when all is not. The US military's daily press briefings are so specious they are known as "feeding the chickens." Every grunt in the field can tell you the public affairs officials are spinning the ground truth till it is shiny and gossamer thin. The officers know the victory narrative is a lie. We are getting out while the getting is good. The diplomats know it. The Taliban fighters sure know it. The same day we dined at the DFAC the Associated Press (AP) ran a story, "Taliban Likens US Pullout to Vietnam Exit." A Taliban spokesman called the American withdrawal from Afghanistan a "'declare victory and run' strategy." The jihadi said, "They just want to flee from Afghanistan just as they turned tail and ran from Vietnam."

American soldiers on a WHAM (winning hearts and minds) mission in eastern Afghanistan. Photo by author.

The sere landscape of Afghanistan that has challenged so many invaders. Photo by author.

The tiny irrigated plots in the vast desert landscape illustrate the importance of water in semiarid Khost Province. Photo by author.

Pashtun tribesmen engaging long-shadowed American soldiers on a WHAM mission. Photo by author.

As security soldiers stand guard against attack, a US Agribusiness Development Team pitches a project to tribesmen under a *shura* (meeting) tree at the edge of Shobo Khel village in Khost Province. Photo by author.

A soldier ponders Afghanistan's rugged Hindu Kush mountains during a Blackhawk flight. Photo by author.

Getting the soldiers' views on a mission in Helmand Province's volatile Nawa District. Courtesy of US Army, photo by Major Denton Smith.

Graffiti spray painted on a US forward operating base's security barrier in embattled Laghman Province. Photo by author.

FIVE

Shoulders

HE'S A SYSTEMS GUY, A WEST POINT GRAD WHO JUST KEEPS coming back to Afghanistan. First this contract, then that—joint command, development, counter-IED, spec ops, he doesn't care. Smart, smart, smart. "Five-pound brain," soldiers say. Mephistopheles beard, intense eyes that bore into you as he lays out the big picture, then the big, big picture, then the small minds that makes it all go bad. Quotes Ben Franklin, "A great empire and little minds go ill together."

We walk across BAF in the cold night air, headed for the PX (post exchange) so I can grab a late dinner at the Pizza Hut. Patches of ice and snow on Disney Drive. Worried about throwing my back out with a war-zone itinerary ahead of me, I step as gingerly as a new fawn. Soldiers on endless auto-salute as streams of officers approach. Grunts hate BAF with all its brass and their inane rules. Out in a beleaguered, bullet-pocked combat outpost, one told me, "I'd rather be beaten with a stick than have to go to BAF."

Bundled up against the cold, people queue at the tiny food counters crammed into the low-ceilinged prefab. Damp, warm, with the smell of grease and coffee, like a remote truck stop in the empty West. Heavy-shouldered soldiers banter at the tables. A slight contractor with lavish eye makeup and a headscarf flirts with a burly contractor, then spins hard-faced for the door. At the Green Beans coffee stand, a small older man with an impeccable Montana hat, khaki field coat, and cowboy boots stands with perfect posture. He glances sharply at me a few times, the florescent lights glinting his wire-rims into twin suns.

A chai latte for the systems guy; a small pepperoni pizza for me. He tells me about his new contract with the Special Operations Command (socom). I tell him about soldiers and contractors saying it's a failed war; about the sergeants who said their long-term was four months. "Naturally, the spec ops people don't think that," he says. "They're professionals. War is their job. They don't want to get involved in politics and issues outside of their mission. They stay focused. socom figures they'll be here long after 2014." An Afghan worker rushes over to our table with a stricken look. We'd accidentally unplugged the large flat-screen television—God forbid a TV should be dark in Little America. Methodic distraction to keep everyone from realizing they're in Afghanistan. A few minutes later, a compact shooter anxiously asks to change the channel.

As a football game blares overhead, the systems guy fumes about the endemic loss of institutional memory. The story of the Afghanistan War: go-getter careerists rotating through with new strategies and policies that nullify hard-won knowledge and negate previous efforts. "I'd mapped out hundreds of IED-prone culverts in 2009, but a sigint (signals intelligence) rotation required all info over two years old to be pulled off the system and be classified," he says. "I had to get permission to get my own data. Had to go to Kabul with a hard drive and hand-carry it back to get the location of the culverts back in the system. It was lost until then." He talks about how many, "maybe 40 percent," of the top US military officers never deploy, so their PowerPoint fantasies are never tempered by the ground truth. About the military's reluctance to put life-saving techniques into the field unless repackaged as expensive military-industrial gear. I ask why he keeps doing it; why he keeps coming back.

His gets his diabolical eyes going; gray, furzed eyebrows in agitato. "You asked why are people out here? This is why: As long as there are a bunch of young kids who want to come out and prove themselves, there needs to be some older guys, like me, to be out here to teach them and protect them from themselves. The other thing is: Do you want to be with the sheep—the people back home—or with the wolves?"

"I get that," I say.

"Then there was this French movie about Dien Bien Phu I saw as a kid," he says. "There were these French paratroopers who parachuted in—even to the last day. When you could look down and see it was obvious that it was lost. Drop missions were aborted because there was nothing left to drop to, and they jumped anyway. Even radio operators and gunners. And I thought, 'That's cool. I want to be one of those people, who jump anyway.' Then there's the poem I remember, that I memorized." And he recited A. E. Housman's WWI poem, "Epitaph on an Army of Mercenaries":

> These, in the day when heaven was falling,
> The hour when earth's foundations fled,
> Followed their mercenary calling,
> And took their wages, and are dead.
>
> Their shoulders held the sky suspended;
> They stood, and earth's foundations stay;
> What God abandoned, these defended,
> And saved the sum of things for pay.

He says, "I used to sign my e-mails with something like 'shoulders holding the sky suspended since whatever,' but nobody ever got it.

"This is it for me," he suddenly tells me. "This is my last rotation here. I've had enough."

We stand in the cold in front of the PX, talking about the fragility of empires, and their inevitable decline. We look around at BAF, eerily quiet in comparison to its wild boom days of 2009. "We are certainly decaying here," he says. He talks about the units in "this retrograde mode," doing nothing but packing. "The PRTs [provincial reconstruction teams], they are just packing up to go. Not doing any projects. Just this packing up shit. And special forces, they're the rear guard. Keeping the lid on while the rest get out." He surveys the darkening fairyland of Bagram around us, and says, "America, it'll last at least through our lifetimes." And we shake hands and go different ways.

SIX

Salerno

THE BLAST FLATTENED THE DINING FACILITY, AT LEAST THE side closest to Forward Operating Base Salerno's high, dirt-filled, wire-and-fabric Hesco walls, where an insurgent had exploded his enormous truck bomb the year before. I'm shocked by the rubble. FOB Salerno's DFAC was made of hardened masonry, supposedly able to take a direct hit. I'd confidently waited out rocket and mortar attacks in there, sipping coffee and waiting for a lull to dash across the base to file dispatches. Thought of it as kinetic surfing: waiting for the moment.

Hunkered down in eastern Afghanistan's Khost Province, Salerno is just a few miles from the wild Pakistani tribal regions. Insurgents attack Salerno so often that the grunts have dubbed the place Rocket City. Afghans in the base haji shops sell black hoodies with "Rocket City" embroidered in blood-red thread.

As I stand at the DFAC with an officer, it's clear the wrecked structure and surrounding destruction repudiates the happy story that security is improving. Salerno is one of the oldest and largest US bases in Afghanistan. It just isn't secure. A large, complex attack this successful is clear evidence that the insurgency remains strong. But ambitious officers need to stick to the victory narrative. The officer looks both ways for eavesdroppers before telling me nine insurgents charged the base with two truck bombs. They breached the outer Hesco barrier with one of the truck bombs, but the inner wall channeled them into a killing zone inside the base. While the FOB's Giant Voice mechanically intoned the dread code for insurgents inside the walls, Apache helicopters hovering above rained down chain-gun fire. "They were shooting down *inside* the base," one

normally phlegmatic sergeant major exclaimed to me. Near the bombed
DFAC, the blast leveled the PX and blew out the stained-glass windows
on one side of the FOB's small chapel. Made the little chapel look off-
balance, half-blind. One US soldier died after a team of military veteri-
narians raced to repel the attack. "They came running," the officer says
as we solemnly assess the damage. "That's what we do."

:   :   :   :   :

The major and I walk into the replacement DFAC, a football-field-sized
clamshell tent. Hundreds of civilians dressed in almost obligatory 5.11
tac clothes are lined up for food and crowding the long tables. I'm used
to the FOB being filled with military. I turn to the major and jokingly ask,
"Where are the soldiers?" And she laughs back. One contractor who
works on Radar Hill later tells me the majority of the five thousand
people on Salerno are now civilian contractors.

As the politicians and generals ratchet down the number of troops
in Afghanistan, they are replacing them with highly paid contractors—
one and a half to two contractors for every withdrawn soldier, with the
proportion rising as the withdrawal progresses. It's perfect Washington-
think: the contractors don't show up on the politically sensitive boots-
on-the-ground count. So the White House can tell Americans that the
United States is withdrawing from Afghanistan, even as the ante goes
up. Despite a congressional mandate to report the numbers of military
contractors in the war zones, the Pentagon keeps the numbers under
wraps long past the reporting deadlines. No one knows how many contractors are in Afghanistan. A lot.

The contractors are a mismatched lot: Retired military men walking
through the DFAC with their upright bearing and double-dipping privilege. At one table, some development pros, former idealists with glib
smiles and cynical eyes, talk shop with a couple of "aid chicks," the term
a USAID official used to describe her development-industry sisters.
Lumpy academics with horn-rims who are hitting the honeypot for contracts that double and triple their university salaries intently eat their
food. The tech and logistics contractors keep to themselves. Some contractors are young, wanting a high-paid adventure to get started. Many

are older, with grim tales of alimony, foreclosure, gambling debts, and drug-addled children, hoping to turn things around with one more high-paid war contract. It's as though postconflict stabilization, aka nation building, has become a twenty-first-century WPA—a War Projects Administration. A make-work project halfway around the world for the already entitled. Except Roosevelt's WPA (Works Progress Administration) left an enduring legacy. This WPA just burns the money.

As we eat our breakfast of oatmeal and fruit in the vast, white-fabric tent, the major hypes the Afghan army improvements, the decrease in insurgent attacks. Fit, informed, funny, she is using the military to educate herself, applying to Georgetown for a master's degree. With her quick mind and perfect composure, she exudes competency. She shows me a picture of her partner, a handsome African American who looks forthrightly into the camera. "She's a professor," the major says proudly. Intent on my food, I scarcely register the siren for incoming when there's the clatter of her metal chair and I see her power-walking for the door at almost cartoon speed, like there should have been a cloud of dust in her wake. I hear a boom. Oh, better go. And I hurry after her, joining the swarm of contractors and soldiers heading for the concrete bunkers. The major is already in the nearby bunker, shooing wide-eyed contractors forward into the middle of the low concrete space, compressing them together to make room for the people behind us. Once everyone is thoroughly packed, she sits down with a sigh. I compliment her on her speed and take-charge attitude. "I've got a lot to live for," she says.

:   :   :   :   :

The horde of contractors is a big change from a few years prior, when thousands of soldiers were rotating through Salerno for full-on counterinsurgency operations. Convoys of armored gun trucks regularly negotiated the FOB's security chicanes on their way to patrol the province. Artillery laid down supporting barrages and dueled with the insurgents in the hills. Twitchy snipers waited for their red-mist moment, when they saw heads exploding in their high-powered scopes. Military and civilian teams were busy trying to nation-build with development and aid projects. Come nightfall, the darkened Humvees of the shadowy spec ops teams rolled out of their sequestered compounds on top-secret missions. "Don't *ever* walk in there," a captain warned me one day when we passed one of the curtain-walled compounds. The gate was open. "Don't even *look* in there," he said.

The spec ops hunter-killer teams were primal, an ugly, dark secret that titillated politicians in excellent suits. Power projection. The teams targeted the infamous JPEL (Joint Prioritized Effects List) of high-value insurgent leaders and technicians. From my time on the ground and published WikiLeaks revelations, I knew spec ops teams had also taken out innocent civilians, like the Afghan women and children killed at Ali Daya in 2009 during a raid gone horribly wrong. A four-day-old baby died from gunshot wounds. After Afghan protests, the US brass thundered in with solatia and condolence payments to ostensibly compensate the tribesmen. I visited the small, dusty village not long after with a military development team tasked with using aid goodies to win hearts and minds. Frisbees, soccer balls, candy, and a generator. That didn't do it either.

One day I needed to hitch a ride on a military helicopter to move to another base. As it turned out, a spec ops team controlled the only helicopters still flying that day. A sergeant major offered to ask the team if they would ferry me. Trudging toward the heavily armed squad squatting beside the landing zone, I could feel my adrenaline kicking in. Bearded, long haired, dressed in ragged tac clothes and dirty *keffiyeh* scarves, the men looked like a collection of malevolent linebackers, gymnasts, and ninjas. Snake eaters. I felt like prey walking into a pack of predators. There was a shimmering menace around them: murderous fury, scarcely restrained. This won't work, I thought. They'll smell it. So I cycled a calming mantra as I stumbled across the rocks with my awkward load toward the world's best assassins. Breathe, I thought, breathe. But the sergeant major, bless him, had more to do with my flying out than my marginally effective breathing techniques did. Intent on getting me on board (and probably out of his hair), he chatted the spec ops sergeants up, admiring their sophisticated weapons and communications gear. Cold, assessing eyes. Fluid moves. After watching me for a while, the commander said, "Hey, are you the *Wall Street Journal* reporter who wants to embed with us?" I wasn't, but he said I could go anyway. As we filed toward the waiting Chinook, a small Japanese American operative with his long black hair twisted into a samurai topknot strode by with a battered, wooden-handled sword hilt sticking out of his pack, where it was convenient to grab.

SEVEN

Retrograde

"NOTHING IS MORE DIFFICULT THAN A RETROGRADE IN contact," the airborne commander growls in a gravely Brooklyn accent. When I ask if "retrograde in contact" is the military definition for retreat, he bristles. "Withdrawal," he snaps, "withdrawal under pressure." And then he smiles a toothy grin like Big Bad Wolf in Grandma's clothes. Battle hardened, hulking, gimpy from decades of jumping out of planes into America's wars, the West Point–educated officer knows the risks of fighting while packing to go. From Alexander the Great's time to the Soviet war, soldiers have fallen while trying to extract themselves from Afghanistan. They just want to go home, but at some point when the troop levels drop, all the remnant force can do is protect itself.

The commander's masonry-hardened brigade headquarters is a windowless maze of makeshift cubicles, offices, and conference rooms with wall-sized PowerPoint screens, where a generation of American officers vainly tried to integrate years of uncoordinated, disconnected, sometimes contradictory operations into elaborate multimedia presentations that showed the chaos was all in the plan. All under control. In the lobby, large framed photos of presidents and defense secretaries and commanders testify to the long American presence here. I remember the adage attributed to Sun Tzu: "Tactics without strategy is the noise before defeat." Overhead I can hear hovering Chinooks. There's a thump of some distant explosion. The urgent rush of forced hot air. Back in Washington, Obama and Hamid Karzai are sparring over post-2014 troop levels and aid money. But on the front lines, retrograde is defining America's endgame in Afghanistan.

On the forward operating bases and combat outposts, palletizing fever is high as soldiers merrily move out (sometimes prematurely as critical equipment disappears into the withdrawal vortex). Development teams are closing down; frontline State Department officers heading to bigger bastions and cushier posts. Hundreds of bases are being decommissioned, many dismantled and "returned to nature," as the officers like to say. Combat Outpost Tillman, named after the NFL football star and special forces soldier Pat Tillman, who died in an infamous friendly fire incident, was one of those closed. "We scraped it clean," the commander exults. I talk to sappers, who traveled north to Tillman to blow up the watchtowers. It was a good moment for them, too. "Blowing up stuff is definitely a cool part of the job," one says brightly. They tell me the army leveled the base into a soccer field, where Afghan boys play a wolfish style of football.

Even Salerno is slated to be bulldozed. "The ANA [Afghan National Army] doesn't have the resources to maintain it," an officer tells me. "And the military doesn't want it to fall into enemy hands, so we are going to return it to the state that we found it when we came to Afghanistan." The US military and GIROA are sparring over the bases. The Pentagon wants to demolish the bases to deprive the jihadis, while GIROA doesn't want to lose all that good booty. Right now, the military is winning. The Afghans can't sustain those wildly unsustainable schools and clinics that USAID and the military built either. Are they going to level them, too?

One night back in my hooch, I read a military logistician's analysis of retrograde. Being twenty-first-century military, he naturally focused on IO: "The first and foremost consideration during a military retrograde is the risk of creating negative images," and he clucked about all the vehicles and weapons that the vanquished Soviets abandoned when they fled. Seemingly more concerned with perception than defeat, the logistician counseled, "Avoid leaving abandoned military equipment and supplies strewn across the countryside that would provide our enemies with a propaganda opportunity."

But the Afghan National Army is still the big question mark. Will the ANA fight without US carrots and sticks? By the Pentagon's metrics, the ANA is an abysmal army, corrupt, rife with deserters and turncoats, essentially ineffective without US handholding. But with 2014 looming,

American commanders are now insisting that their Afghan counterparts take over the fight. "We kind of gave it a 'tough love' approach," the commander rumbled. "We told the Afghans, 'You've got to do it at some point.' We've gone from a partnered role to advise and assist."

The US military's "Shohna ba Shohna" (shoulder-to-shoulder) partnering strategy has abruptly given way to an "After you" attitude. Cold turkey. The commander tells of denying Afghan calls for air and artillery support during engagements; of Afghan casualties being trucked to basic Afghan clinics rather than being helicoptered to high-tech US combat hospitals; of even refusing cossetted Afghan commanders the air transport they were used to demanding—and getting. "We fly them nowhere," the commander emphasizes with a knock on the table. "It's a big transition, but it had to happen. It's a clash of wills. We tell them, 'You can do it. Your ancestors had the will.'"

The commander talks about the 352,000 Afghan national security forces spread across the country. I ask how the Afghan army is doing in his sector of eastern Afghanistan. "Across the AO [area of operations], I wouldn't paint a rosy picture," he says, "frustration to satisfaction. We've had some very good success. We've had some moderate success." He looks at me and says firmly, "We have not encountered any nightmares."

The Afghan insurgents aren't dumb. They keep up steady, economical attacks. IEDs continue to be their weapon of choice. Complex attacks by a small number of fighters, such as the ones launched on Kabul, BAF, Salerno, and Camp Bastion when Prince Harry was there. Efficiently broadcast through the international media, the attacks advertise that the insurgency is still thriving. And the jihadis bide their time.

While I am on the FOB, the PAOs tout statistics that show a drop in insurgent attacks, though the metrics don't seem to fit the picture of relentless pressure that soldiers and contractors keep describing. As it turns out, they don't. Not long after, the AP caught the military in "a record-keeping error": the army statisticians left out insurgent attack reports from the ANA. The revised figures showed attacks are still increasing, though at a slowing rate of growth. Military officers know a slowing increase in attacks can have multiple causes. And more importantly, most know the special forces maxim: "If an insurgency isn't shrinking, it's winning." The Taliban-led insurgency has grown at a double-digit rate every year since the US invasion.

Insiders earlier posited to me that the (misreported) attack decline actually reflected a de facto truce with the Taliban. In their view, casualty-cautious US officers ordered fewer combat patrols, which meant the penned-up US soldiers encountered lower numbers of Taliban IEDs and ambushes. And the insurgents were OK with the stalemate, because their shadow officials were effectively governing the hinterlands. A win-win.

I ask the commander about the idea. Ever the warrior (and deft spokesman), the commander challenges the idea that US soldiers are not "out there," because he says they are constantly on the roads with retrograde convoys, as though withdrawal and combat operations are the same thing. "We're not finding the mother lodes of caches [insurgent military supplies] when we go out," he insists. "We're not getting a fight." He pauses. "I thought there'd be a lot more action—sophistication, lethality, coordinated attacks. Haven't seen it. I expected a much more kinetic environment," he tells me with a trace of disappointment. Soldiers want their war. Then I ask about the assessment that Afghan insurgents are just husbanding their forces until the United States withdraws in 2014. "Husbanding of forces," he responds quickly. "I might buy that."

EIGHT

Better

THERE IT IS, A YELLOW BOMB SHOVED INTO THE MIDDLE OF A culvert. Lying in Afghanistan's moon dust, I stare at the plastic palm-oil bucket with its taped-on paraphernalia, an IED ready to blow us to kingdom come. On the road above me, I can hear the Afghan soldier in his armored bomb suit scuffling along, sweeping, sweeping with his beeping Vallon mine detector. In the previous four years, IEDs have accounted for about two-thirds of all ISAF (International Security Assistance Force) and Afghan security forces casualties. And there it is: a big yellow homemade bomb. Extremely cheap, extremely effective, extremely lethal. A cold, bright day, and there I am, looking at the end of days.

I clamber up onto the road. The ANA soldier is flat in the dirt, the mine detector beside him, his spaceman helmet intently focused on the road. I hold my breath as his ungloved hand ever so gently probes a lump. An American suddenly calls out, "You know, you've already been blown up three times." And the captain points to the fake IEDs implanted in the road and rock wall we just passed. "You're dead," he yells.

The ANA counter-IED training course at Camp Parsa is "tough love" in the flesh. With 2014 looming, the United States needs the ANA to also take over the anti-IED fight. I am watching American soldiers mentor a route clearance company of ninety Afghan soldiers, whose mission is to locate and disable IEDs before the bombs do their heinous job. It's a six-week crash course. "We partner up," the American captain assures me, "share our best practices. At this point, these trainers require minimal assistance." When we walk up to the class not far from the culvert, the Afghan soldiers are squatting on the bare yellow plain in front of a blackboard with IED diagrams. The major jokes with the American captain, "How did you get them to do that? All of them, in rows, paying attention." The captain laughs and said they *are* getting better. A beat. *Really*. The Afghan counter-IED troops, mostly Tajiks from the north, look like sad sacks, like they know they have been sent to the very worst unit in the very worst place to do the very worst job. Woeful. The Afghan officers seem crisp and intent—but then again the officers don't have to go probing for bombs with bare hands.

Oh, yeah, equipment. The captain tells me the Afghan units are "appropriately equipped" for the counter-IED mission. "A lot of the equipment is very, very similar," he insists, perhaps a little too earnestly. But the devil is in the details. US forces are primarily using up-to-date Duke jammers to negate remote electronic detonators, such as cell phones. But the ANA has to make do with earlier iterations of electronic countermeasure equipment, such as Symphony, which work—sort of. There are reasons the US troops stopped using the older technology. The training and sustainability issues are always cropping up. An American engineer complains the ANA soldiers burn up their jammers, because they forget to turn them off when they stop their trucks. "Fried 'em," he says. Can the Afghan army keep fighting the American way after the United States splits? Before I even ask about spare parts, the captain launches into a discourse about all the spare parts the corrupt Afghan commanders are hiding. "They're always wanting more. They don't need more." In place of the robots and sophisticated mechanical arms that the US counter-IED teams use to remotely probe for bombs from the relative safety of their armored trucks, the Afghans use their eyes and "the patented Afghan clearing rod," as the captain flippantly terms it. "It's a twenty-foot-long pole with a rake on it." I hear tales of Afghan soldiers picking up live IEDs and carrying them into their compounds to store. "The ANSF [Afghan National Security Forces] have no rules for explosives," one grunt says. And instead of the robustly armored MRAP vehicles that protect American soldiers, the ANA counter-IED units tool around in thin-skinned vehicles. Behind the troops, I can see a lineup of battered old Humvees, pickups, even motorcycles. Gives me a shiver. I've spoken with US military doctors who treat ANA soldiers with horrific wounds suffered in their vulnerable vehicles. I've seen the black triage tent where the worst casualties are taken to die.

It's not surprising that one-third of the Afghan security forces have to be replaced every year. Two to 3 percent of the Afghan soldiers and police desert every month. Ghost soldiers fill up the ranks, fighters who only exist on paper so their corrupt commanders can nab the internationally funded salaries.

"We're not partnering now," the captain says. "The last unit out cut the ties. We're absolutely an 'advise and assist' with this route clearance company." There it is—tough love. The captain says that one way or another, the Afghans are doing the counter-IED job. He stands shoulder to shoulder with the Afghan company commander, a short, grizzled Tajik with a fierce look and a cocky beret. The Afghan officer stands at attention, glowering, mute as the American captain speaks with can-do conviction: "They've improved greatly over the last three years. They've never failed to complete a mission due to operational failure." He pauses, and looks to the horizon. "The ANA, it's underdeveloped," he says quietly to me. "It's undeniable."

NINE

Boom

WE BEGIN WITH A PRAYER, "HEAVENLY FATHER, WATCH OVER us as we go out on this mission," and then the combat engineers climb into their heavily armored RG-31 MRAP. We are part of a US Army RCP (Route Clearance Package) convoy of counter-IED vehicles: the RG-31, the hefty Huskies with their ground-penetrating radar, a mammoth anti-IED Buffalo, and a gargantuan armored wrecker—for when all the anti-IED technology fails. The vehicles look crusty, cobbled together, like they were bought off the surplus lot of the first *Star Wars* movie. The mission is to patrol the road out to Lakan, an ANA post at the ragged edge of Khost. A bunch of American boys looking for buried bombs.

After tens of thousands of insurgent bombs changed the wars in Iraq and Afghanistan, the US military reacted with a revved-up counter-IED war. In the military argot, there is left of boom and there is right of boom. Left of boom is prebomb, where intel and spooks mesh human and electronic intelligence with roadside-bomb databases to try to untangle the IED webs that connect financiers, smugglers, bomb makers, and the insurgents who plant the mines, and then neutralize them before the boom. Right of boom is what happens when left of boom fails. Right of boom includes the bomb that blew you and whatever happened to be around into pieces, and then the forensics to try to understand the boom, and the subsequent technology to combat it. The technology includes the armored V-hulled MRAPs, the behemoth counter-IED vehicles, mine-detection equipment, jammers of startling sophistication, robots, eagle-eyed spy dirigibles, groin-protecting armored underwear, and the frontline traumatic brain injury (TBI) clinics to treat soldiers devastated by the IED pressure blasts—"the invisible wounds of war," the flacks called them. So my road clearance package is definitely right of boom.

"We have one historic IED area," the young RCP captain explains over the crackling intercom as we wind through the security chicanes toward the highway. "We're the ones up front looking for bombs, reducing them, and letting follow-on forces get on with their mission," he says. "The bad guys are mainly targeting the ANSF these days," he explained, adding that Americans still get their share of bombs. Talking about the RCP vehicles' ability to survive large IEDs, he says, "We can handle up to sixty-pounders. Had some strikes, but the guys walk away—shaken but not stirred."

The RCP patrol is a strapped-in MRAP ride across a sere landscape—the company's 256th mission in its four months in Khost. Though most US soldiers are tightly restricted to the bases, the RCP patrols are breaking the wire in record-breaking numbers. We are traveling through a rolling brown landscape, punctuated with walled farm compounds, *qalats*. Rounded mountains rise in the distance. We pass the Afghan farmers walking beside their fields of greening wheat, and then drive through mud-walled villages. Lime-green pepper trees and stalls filled with red and green vegetables line the road.

"Pretty much what we're looking for is anything, plastic bags, yellow jugs, suspicious locals," the captain tells me. Overhead, Apache helicopters reconnoiter the route. The radio crackles with the Apache's report, "We have massed military-age men at coordinates . . . ." The radio chatter then went on to notate the enumerated coordinates, which I don't have. Driving along a trash-strewn lane, the driver calls out, "I can see why they put IEDs in plastic bags—they're everywhere." There is a whir as the GeoCam on the truck's thirty-foot-long articulated mechanical arm ratchets high in the air to scout for ambushes. "It's got the shakes," the operator complains. "They probably miscalibrated this after the tire and axle got blown to smithereens." The video monitor is blotched with purple and yellow, then red and yellow, then baby blue. Soon there's a burning smell. "I think it's the gyro," the operator says.

For the most part, the insurgents are winning the IED battle. There are still thousands of bombs emplaced each year, and far too many do their job. When IEDs became a game changer in Iraq, the military established JIEDDO (Joint Improvised Explosive Device Defeat Organization) in 2006 to combat the roadside bombs. But developing effective detection techniques has been elusive, especially in Afghanistan, where IEDs are most often made of a few simple elements and farm fertilizer, rather than the unused artillery shells of the Iraqi insurgents. After JIEDDO got scorched in a scathing GAO (Government Accountability Office) report in 2010, Secretary of Defense Robert Gates ordered a high-level team called C-SIG (cross-cutting, senior-level group) to "harmonize" the anti-IED efforts in Afghanistan, where the booms just keep getting bigger.

Down the road a bit, the truck stops as the articulated arm snakes into a culvert, the GeoCam nosing around for IEDs. Prime IED real estate, culverts are the pucker place for almost every convoy I am on in Afghanistan. To prevent insurgents from emplacing the bombs, the US military fields an array of culvert-denial systems. "We've got some good systems in place," the captain says when I ask about them. Then he says, "That was a big thing a few years ago. You have to know if they've been tampered with." Ongoing oversight of the installed culvert covers is the perennial missing link. But even the installation needs critical oversight that often doesn't happen. The Special Inspector General for Afghanistan Reconstruction (SIGAR) reported that Afghan contractors fail to properly install culvert-denial devices, in some cases failing to even install them. Cold comfort as we cross another culvert. Pucker place.

The captain gripes about the insurgents' hoax bombs, empty containers connected to old cell phones that tie up tens of millions of dollars of military assets for extended periods. "It doesn't take much," he says. I can imagine those rascal jihadis Aziz and Mohammad cracking up as they reminisce about the traffic jam of multi-million-dollar American vehicles gathered around their discarded palm-oil bucket with Haji's broken cell phone taped to the side. "Oh, the helicopters up there—how many? How many? How much do *they* cost? Oh, Aziz. The Americans."

It's a long crawl across an ancient landscape. Stream-of-conscious truck-banter eases the time: The eighteen IEDs the insurgents laid in one route. Route clearance patrol for a nighttime raid to capture an IED leader—"incredibly difficult to clear at night". The loss of two mine rollers and an engine block. "Two hours of seat-of-the-pants insanity," the captain terms it. Their lucky driver, a Hispanic who's "never been rocked."

The relative dangers of various IEDs; the relative comfort of counter-IED vehicles (the six-wheel, fifty-six-thousand-pound Buffalo with reclining seats and high-volume air conditioning is "a Cadillac"). The "crazy" American helicopter pilot who used their truck to practice strafing runs. The ANA counter-IED teams that do it the Afghan way—"no rules." An "exceptionally fresh" dead goat beside the road, notable because insurgents sometimes hide bombs in the carcasses.

It is comforting to travel on a counter-IED mission with a band of engineers, solid, literal, phlegmatic engineers. That is good. I don't need any dramatics, don't need anyone to embellish. I asked an RCP engineer one day what they called IEDs that were so powerful they could crack an MRAP like an egg, could wreak devastation that flashed churning fear into most soldiers. I asked, "What do you call the really big ones? A two-hundred-pounder? When you find a really big IED, what do you call it? What's the name you guys use?" He looked at me blankly for a few seconds, and then said, "We say, uh, that's a really big one."

We finally reach Lakan, a dusty Hesco-ed and razor-wired outpost in a bleak khaki landscape near the Pakistani border. With its defensive walls and large guard towers, Lakan looks like the medieval fortress of a very minor baron. An Afghan government flag hangs limply on the ramparts. There are no ANA soldiers to be seen, no comradely salutes from the guardhouses. This is clearly an expendable outpost deep in Taliban country. As the convoy executes a complicated turnaround in front of the fort, there is some tension. "Vulnerable," comes over the intercom. I watch a motorcyclist approach at a good clip, a bearded man in a turban. "Eyes on," someone says. Suicide bomber? No worry. The Afghan scarcely glances at the convoy as he drives by with an AK-47 strapped on his back. "It's a successful day," the captain says, "if we all come home."

TEN

WHAM

ZABUL PROVINCE IS ON FIRE, BUT THE AMERICAN FARMER-soldiers have flies on their minds. Sitting in a hardened structure, the military agricultural specialists are talking about the flies in the new US-financed slaughterhouse. Built in the provincial capital of Qalat City to curry favor with a corrupt Afghan politician, the expensive new abattoir was constructed by USAID in connivance with beltway bandit Chemonics. The slaughterhouse is getting little use—in part because the tile floor has a raised pattern that holds blood and debris. "Wall of flies," the National Guard veterinarian says disgustedly. "The design," he sneers, his deep bass voice resonating disapproval. He shakes his head and rolls his eyes. "No fluid drainage. No power. Bad location. No respect for local customs. No inspection. No enforcement." The other soldiers nod vigorously. "Blood and flies," one adds.

The soldiers are textbook counterinsurgency warriors, using development projects to theoretically woo Afghan farmers from the insurgents. We sit chatting in a windowless concrete room with overstuffed Pakistani furniture and a thermos of green Afghan tea in fortified Forward Operating Base Smart. Sitting near their weapons and body armor, the ag specialists seem like some hybrid species of extreme extension agents. In civilian life, the burly African American veterinarian is an animal science professor in Mississippi, but now he's a sergeant in an agribusiness development team (ADT) on a nation-building mission in Afghanistan. But the vet knows slaughterhouses, and he knows flies. And he knows this development isn't winning any Afghan hearts and minds.

WHAM is the inevitable military acronym for "winning hearts and minds," the tainted phrase that dates back to America's failed counterinsurgency in Vietnam and has somehow persisted into the Afghanistan War. Soldiers talk about going on WHAM missions—and they aren't even being ironic. WHAM in Afghanistan covers a broad spectrum of US-financed development programs that sound excellent on the surface. The enormously expensive programs are supposed to deliver aid and reconstruction, and in the process facilitate nation building, rule of law, good government, human rights, and women's empowerment. Ostensibly transformational, most of the programs are systemically exploited by the malign networks that connect ambitious American careerists and corporations with corrupt Afghan insiders and the insurgents. The UN estimates that the Taliban is skimming somewhere between 10 and 20 percent of the international money that pours into Afghanistan. Everybody is in on the take. Everybody wins—except the American taxpayers, the soldiers on the ground, and the benighted Afghans.

Development is a tough mission in Zabul Province. The whole province is insecure. Sitting astride strategic Route One in southeastern Afghanistan, Zabul is critical to the US-led coalition's military efforts. But most of the hinterland's 2,500 remote villages are Taliban controlled, particularly in the high mountains of the north. Sharing a forty-mile-long border with Pakistan, Zabul's barren southern desert is an insurgent gateway. Even the Afghan allies aren't trustworthy. The epidemic of "green on blue" attacks by Afghan soldiers on American troops began a year earlier at nearby Camp Eagle, where an Afghan soldier opened fire on US soldiers at a soccer field.

It takes a full-scale mission for the ADT to travel the few miles across Qalat City from their home base to the ag specialists at FOB Smart. Before we leave, the security officer briefs that there have been eleven security incidents in the previous days, that Route One is on red alert, that TICs (troops in combat) are increasing. The medic straps an individual first aid kit on my body armor. "You got to help someone," he says, "use theirs. Keep yours for you." Asks my blood type. Give me three extra tourniquets to stuff in my pockets. "If you're bleeding out, someone may not want to use one of theirs." We travel in a convoy of MRAPs with machine gunners in the turrets and a mine roller at the lead. Anti-RPG netting covers the gun trucks' armored hides. The thick bulletproof glass is cracked and pocked. The MRAP doors battle-lock shut with a weighty hissing finality. There's air cover overhead for the ADT convoy's race through the ramshackle little capital of Qalat City, around the ratty little roundabout with its rusting scrap-metal sculpture, into the welcoming walls of FOB Smart. A sigh of relief. The ground truth: this is Taliban-controlled country. Anyone who says otherwise is delusional or a truth-spinning sycophant.

Zabul has been a rough post for millennia. Alexander's Castle, a giant fortified hill that Alexander the Great's army erected over two thousand years ago, stands high over Qalat City, a constant reminder of the problems that world conquerors face in Afghanistan. After proto-Afghan tribesmen tied up half of Alexander's infantry and 95 percent of his cavalry in this one small corner of his empire, he is said to have observed, "Afghanistan, easy to march into; hard to march out of."

In the 1890s the British used Alexander's Castle as a redoubt before the Afghans chased them out of Zabul. In the perky capitalist world of the American era, an Afghan entrepreneur started a summit-top restaurant as part of the $10 million US-funded New Qalat City construction project, another chimerical development scheme that collapsed into a ghost town. The restaurant failed, too.

In the conference room, the ADT soldiers segue between war and farming—"bullets and beans," one calls it. They talk about animal husbandry, farmer co-ops, almonds, raisins, the shimmering potential of pomegranates, drip irrigation, rust-resistant wheat seed, beekeeping, animal health, and orchard projects. And the challenges of trying to do aid work in an active war zone. A security sergeant briefs about a recent bike bomb, a BBIED (bicycle-borne improvised explosive device), that detonated near FOB Smart. He talks about another threat aimed at them. "Local Taliban commander tried to emplace an IED targeted at us." So much for winning hearts and minds with farm aid.

An ADT security grunt talks about terror and interdependence: "We stopped twenty meters from a big IED. Just off Route One. We got lucky that day. Made me think. Made it real. Me and lieutenant had a prayer and drove on. Taught me how to man up. You got your boys. You have to do, or something is going to fall apart."

The Mississippians are like a lot of soldiers from the National Guard and reserves that are in Afghanistan, enduring wrenching sacrifice to do their jobs. Solid Americans, bedrock Americans, citizen soldiers. Cops and teachers and managers; the neighbor changing your tire, taking care of your kid, writing your will, looking up your title, sitting beside you in the pew. Young people from one-stoplight or no-stoplight towns, from inner-city neighborhoods, from declining postwar suburbs. Families back home. But here they are, transported from succulent, green Mississippi to arid, brown Afghanistan. It's cold at 5,500 feet, with a vicious wind whipping the sand. Standing in the relentless southern Afghan wind one day, a corporal drawls, "Last time I heard that, it was tornados."

The soldiers grasp for evidence that they are making a difference. One officer tells me, "The Afghans are very sensitive to the sacrifices we have made to help them. They say, the Americans only have one or two sons, but they send them to help us."

A security sergeant brags about little kids and ancient tribesmen giving them high fives when they were doing WHAM work in the villages. He is short and slight, intense, with burr-cut white-blond hair. He leads the MRAP convoy through the base to the gate, walking with a gunfighter swagger, prompting the brawny black gunner to say over the intercom, "If the sergeant be two feet taller, he'd be *bad*. He's got the walk." The security sergeant loves being in the military, but is straining to believe they have a doable mission. In the conference room, he says, "In a way, the military is not suited to do this, but there's no one else."

Reminds me of Slim Charles, the character in David Simon's *The Wire*, telling his drug gang, "Don't matter who did what to who at this point. Fact is, we went to war, and now there ain't no going back. I mean, shit, it's what war is, you know? Once you in it, you in it. If it's a lie, then we fight on that lie. But we gotta fight."

The soldiers are increasingly soured, conflicted, confused. They want to go home. A young African American soldier shows me a picture of her radiant brown baby, and says, "Just from a mother's perspective, there's no place like home. No place like home. I need to be home with my baby."

More tea, a dish of pistachios and one with hard candies, some withered green raisins. A couple of security soldiers lounge by the entrance into the hall. A few development officials from the PRT (provincial reconstruction team) wander in. Hybrid military-civilian teams organized to do aid and development work in active war zones, the PRTs were hearts-and-minds warriors with a lot of security. Often odd and discordant amalgams of military, diplomats, aid workers, and assorted development specialists, the PRTs were a major element in the US counterinsurgency strategy. Leaning against one of the masonry walls, the PRT commander talks about Afghan officials "depending on the kindness of strangers," calling them "the Scarlett O'Haras of Afghanistan"— which confuses me until I realize he means Blanche DuBois. A smart guy trying to do an impossible job, he talks about confronting avaricious Afghan officials with "uncomfortable firmness."

With the development money drying up, so is the American officials' power to control mostly corrupt Afghan officials. "The GIROA officials are showing little interest since funding is coming to a close," one officer tactfully says. The group laughs derisively. One officer said the US-funded aid being channeled through the Ministry of Agriculture in Kabul never makes it to the provincial level, as it is stolen high above. Another complains about the US-supplied wheat seed that the provincial director sucked up: "We thought the DAIL [Director of Agriculture, Irrigation, and Livestock] had planted the wheat seed." The commander says, "We've done about all the good we can do with the DAIL." The ADT has focused on education, rather than development projects that corrupt officials can easily fleece. It causes tension. The Afghan officials want the money. The veterinarian reaches for his teacup and laughs, "I told one Afghan official that I was bringing knowledge. The official said, 'We can use that, too.'"

The soldiers detail the everyday realities of retrograde and its implications for the counterinsurgency. MRAP problems are grounding the ADT. Rushed design. Parts shortages. Mechanics rotating out. "It's just a never-ending problem to keep our trucks running," the commander says. They speak of aid and development funding being drastically cut, including the great slush fund of Commander's Emergency Response Program (CERP) money that funded almost a decade of unsustained and unsustainable projects. "The slaughterhouse is not in use. The stockyard project is canceled," an officer says. It's endgame, nearing the finale, almost the end of the show. But it's a bad show that has gone on far too long. The players are tired and ready to go home. No juice, no energy. Just shuffling along till the last number. It just hasn't come together. The commander concludes, "The stuff we're doing are small victories. Some days we wonder why we're here, to be honest. We're just trying to do some good."

The commander's soft north Mississippi accent makes his statements seem elegiac in that sad, southern lost-cause way. He says, "The US military and the State Department and USDA [United States Department of Agriculture] and other agencies have definitely given this country a chance to form a government, to form an army, to form a police department, and to provide some kind of governance to the people. There's no doubt about that. The time that's been spent, the money, the lives—they've had the opportunity. They've had plenty of years of 'side by side.' Now it's up to them. It's their country and they need to decide how they want to run it." The commander concludes, "The fundamental thing is we're paying them to help themselves. It's just frustrating."

Like a lot of officers I encounter, the commander is desperately trying to reconcile his sense of duty with a contempt for the extravagant counterinsurgency that is propping up a feckless, predatory Afghan government. They see crazy aid largesse in Afghanistan, while their families back home are struggling. I hear stories of officers leaving the service, seeking counseling to try to resolve their cognitive dissonance; to heal their sucker-punched despair.

:   :   :   :   :

Then I ask the ADT soldiers about the earlier slaughterhouse that the United States built in Qalat City. What happened to that one? The one before this one? The officers look at one another with pop-eyed surprise. One asks, "How did you know there was an earlier one?" I reply that there is almost *always* an earlier one that failed. The officer sheepishly admits, "Yeah, we didn't know about the other slaughterhouse till this one was built." A team five years earlier had built a slaughterhouse in Qalat City, but it failed and was forgotten.

Whether a slaughterhouse, school, or clinic, it seems soldiers are forever telling me about an earlier one that was built with absurd amounts of US money and hoopla, then abandoned, then forgotten, and then re-built again as America's counterinsurgency machine rolled on with an ever-new cast of characters who wanted to spice up their CVs. Got to do projects. Got to spend the budget; burn the money. But no follow-up, no sustainability. A slaughterhouse in Ghazni became the local dog-fighting ring. A spec ops officer told me about a USAID-built teacher-training institute that became "Taliban U." When a hard drive crashed, the provincial reconstruction team in Khost Province lost the locations of an entire chain of veterinarian clinics that an earlier team had built. No backup; no institutional memory; no idea where the clinics were located. When someone finally found a hard copy, most of the clinics were looted. In one village, the entire building was gone. Soldiers talked about US-financed schools that were commandeered as homes, even brothels. A State Department officer who did WHAM work with a PRT in Iraq told me his personal record was four schools, four schools that the United States had sequentially built, forgotten about, and replaced.

As the Mississippians relate their lives as Americans in a strange land, I begin taking pictures of the veterinarian, who sits in the large stuffed chair like a wise, imperious Buddha. A commotion suddenly erupts just outside the metal meeting-room door. A scuffling, a metallic clang from the walkway. An American command voice bellows, "Get your fucking hands up! Get your fucking hands up! Drop it, NOW!" A quavering Afghan voice answers. The American again bellows. Green on Blue? A suicide bomber just outside the flimsy metal door? A lightning alertness. Ag specialists now soldiers. Handguns out, they rush to the door. The vet moves fast, like a nimble football lineman. Weapons ready, glancing at one another, nodding assent, hand reaching for the knob, pulsing to erupt through the door and join the fight. Camera still in hand, I am by the hall door where a soldier directed me. I'm about to snap a photo when I remember the flash is still on. Uh, not a good idea—flash, guns, wired soldiers—not good. I am expecting a monster of fire and molten metal to roar into the room. The soldiers count down. One, two, hand now on knob, eyes locked, nodding, nodding, and suddenly a third voice barks outside. It's another US soldier, critiquing the training—very realistic training, as it turns out. Threat nullified, the soldiers shrug, holster their sidearms and resume talking about farming. WHAM in Afghanistan.

ELEVEN

Luck

WE ALL CARRY LUCKY CHARMS. GET TO KNOW A SOLDIER, AND he'll haul out his lucky charms to show you. Picture of the wife, holy medal, Grandma's gold cross, kid's art, auspicious coin, hometown talisman, Dad's dog tags that survived Vietnam—almost always carried close to the heart. On the base, there's an unbuttoning that goes on before they can get at it. Out in the field, there's a ripping sound of Velcro as they scrabble inside their armor. Either way, the charm never leaves their hands as I admire their cherished memento. They light up as they tell me about their special amulet. One grunt carries a pacifier, dropped into his duffel by his baby son, who felt he needed the comfort of one, too. I remember a very tough sniper's tender look as he gazed at his daughter's laminated little crayon drawing.

Afghanistan is the 360-degree war. Danger is all around you, all the time. Random. No front line. No release from the tension. The unrelenting unpredictability of it all. It's all OK, all OK, and then bang! Somehow the lucky charms seem to balance that out.

After seeing the soldiers' love tokens the first time I embedded in Afghanistan, I felt charm deprived. So before going back, I called on loved ones. Very small and very light, I requested; I do have to haul this stuff up mountains. I promised to come back in good health. Just to be sure, most people demanded I return their charm to them personally.

So I travel through Afghanistan with a mixed bag of talismans: My musician son Dylan's lucky drum key; youngest son Seth's Seattle Marathon medal. (Both insist on hand-returns. I imagine the chunks of metal deflecting a bullet.) Grandchildren's drawings. One sister got a retrograde priest to bless a Saint Christopher medal. While I thought Saint Chris was tossed out of the saint corps decades before, the priest insisted he'd been reinstated. This trip I doubled up on Saint Chris, as a dear friend sent a gold medal her mother gave her as a baby. A miscellanea of friends' charms: buckeyes, one in a velvet bag, the other with a particularly large eye; a Hoosier acorn; a well-rubbed Lake Michigan rock; a JFK fifty-cent piece; a "Gratitude and Attitude" medal; one crystal-and-gold earring that needed to be returned to remake the pair her father gave her; a pewter cross; a Thai Buddhist *namol* amulet; three Tibetan prayer medals; a *paladhik* Shiva lingam to protect me from dogs and snakes; a Wiccan charm; an all-seeing Eye of Osiris; fool's gold; a Santo Expedito card (token of Brazilians' favorite instant-miracle saint); a small sky-blue bag with an Iemanja, Goddess of the Sea, traveler's protection; a miniature American flag. As I embed across Afghanistan, soldiers add to my ziplock bag of charms: detachment patches, unit coins, a hand-woven survival wristband.

Charmed, I feel charmed. Just hope my luck holds out.

TWELVE

Shitholes

THE LATRINE IS BRIGHT WHITE AND CLEAN TO A FAULT, AN almost garish contrast to the dark, hardscrabble forward operating base just beyond the metal doors. The two young soldiers are shaving at the long line of sinks and mirrors. One says, "Man, I had a dream last night I was in the shithole." His buddy retorts, "What do you mean 'dream'?"

Like the DFACs at the other end of the alimentary process, latrines are important places in the lives of US soldiers and their fellow travelers. In some ways, latrines define the base's degree of difficulty. On the remote combat outposts, showers are seldom more than a once-a-week douse with a jerry-rigged shower. The outhouses are often plywood, hand-built extra big so soldiers can shit while wearing their body armor. Sewage disposal is a fifty-five-gallon burn-drum with a woebegone grunt stirring the fire with a wooden stick.

On the bigger FOBs, the facilities are more upscale: Porta Potties near the housing and flush latrines and showers within a quarter mile or so. The Porta Potties have their own special Afghanistan challenges: snakes, spiders, and hyenas. Afghanistan is home to poisonous cobras and saw-scaled vipers, and there are plenty of (perhaps apocryphal) stories of finding them in the johns. There are also hair-raising stories of giant camel spiders in the latrines. The mildly poisonous arachnids can grow up to eight inches long, and have a top speed of ten miles per hour, but in the grunt lore, the spiders are the size of footballs and scream as they leap at thirty miles per hour toward your face. Makes opening the door of a Porta Potty a little tense. A sergeant major tells me to be careful using the Porta Potty at night, because that's when the striped hyenas scavenge the trashcans beside the john. Guess they get possessive about their finds.

There are Western-style sitting Porta Potties and Local National Only (aka Afghan) squatting Porta Potties. Lest someone not get the idea, a forward-facing footprint is molded into the plastic on each side of the Local National Only holes. Vive la difference, though there are cross-cultural issues: Soldiers complain about Afghans squatting on the Western-style toilet seats. There are signs in the latrines: "No Standing on Toilets." And then there are the rocks. Afghans typically use rocks to wipe themselves. Makes sense, given that Afghanistan has far more rocks than trees to make toilet paper. A standard rural Afghan outhouse has a carefully chosen collection of nice smooth rocks for the patrons' use. But on the US posts, the rocks play havoc with the contractors' sewage trucks that relentlessly cruise the bases cleaning out the latrines. Many a pump was chewed up by Afghan rocks before the honey dippers figured out a strategy.

As a people, Afghans are extremely modest and fastidious. And they find farting to be extremely embarrassing and shameful. There's an Afghan folktale about a man who accidentally passed gas in front of his family and left home in disgrace for twenty years. When he finally returned home, he paused beside the front door. He heard his wife berating his children to never be farters like their father. So he left for another twenty years. I heard one very dignified Afghan diplomat exhorting a group of US military officers about to deploy to Afghanistan, "Do not fart! The Afghans will be disrespected! Do not fart!" The officers looked at one another. This was bending over backward to win hearts and minds, but OK. In August 2011, the marines' anti-wind-breaking policy became breaking news when a new order banned audible farting in Afghanistan. Semper fidelis, indeed.

Out in the field on missions, the female soldiers, civilian officials, and contractors face a challenge. In unpopulated areas, male soldiers can use shielding bushes and wadis to relieve themselves, and in conservative Afghan villages, grunts can always climb into the MRAPs to use one of the ubiquitous empty water bottles or piddle packs, the plastic urinary-collection devices equipped with deodorant-soaked sponges. But the female soldiers operating in the gender-segregated tribal areas have to be very careful. Hence, the FUD, the female urinary device, designed to facilitate easy STP (stand-to-pee) empty-water-bottle operations. A funnel that a woman holds over her vulva, the FUD, or "weenis," is essential gear for most American women who break the wire. "It's my artificial weenie," one straightforward medic tells me. "I just carry a sheet with me and throw it over my head if I have to go in the MRAPs. I tell the soldiers they can watch if they want, but they won't see anything."

On the forward operating bases, my early morning drill is to throw on some clothes, grab my towel, toiletries, water bottle for brushing teeth, the night's piss bottles (empty water bottles being the soldiers' preferred chamber pot), and head for the latrine in the cold darkness. One morning I am stiff and sore from a mission the day before, so stumble half-asleep across the broken rocks toward the latrine, the water bottle in one pocket of my jacket, a piss bottle in the other. Stop outside the latrine to toss my piss bottle in the dumpster. Hits the bottom with a satisfying thud. Walk into the brightly lit latrine and stash my toilet kit and water bottle in a cubby to go take a shower. Shower (hot water!) and grab my razor, toothbrush, and water bottle from the cubby and head to the lineup of sinks. Almost awake. It's going to be OK. Next up: ibuprofen and breakfast. Sidle past a soldier and put my stuff on the shelf above the sinks. I look up and there is my glowing yellow bottle of pee endlessly reflected in the mirrors. Had tossed the wrong bottle.

THIRTEEN

Road

ROUTE ONE IS A RIBBON, CURLING SLENDER AND BLACK through the rounded, brown hills. The sun struggles through a yellow haze. "This is the part I don't like," the security sergeant says. "It's like the wild, wild West." He calls out, "Dismount on left," and the gunner replies, "Roger, eyes on," as the turret ratchets toward the walking Afghan.

Route One used to be called the Ring Road, about 1,400 miles of two-lane blacktop that connects Afghanistan's major cities. We are in southern Zabul, part of the critical 315-mile-long Kabul-to-Kandahar stretch. If there is any hope of holding on, GIROA and the Americans have to keep the Kabul–Kandahar highway open. Between the crumbling road and the Taliban, it's an almost insurmountable challenge.

During his frantic reelection push after the botched Iraq invasion, President George W. Bush decided that refurbishing the Ring Road on a yeehaw schedule in 2003 would show Afghans how things were done the American way. Well, it did. The highway is infamous for its poor construction and extravagant price. The Louis Berger Group used Bush's election-driven building frenzy to get the road construction requirements substantially reduced—"de-scoped" in development speak—so they could crank out a lousy highway at maximized profits. "Afghan good-enough" is the cynical phrase for bad development, and not many years after the road was finished we are bumping across ruts cut deep into the skimpy asphalt and poorly constructed roadbed. One pothole looks big enough to swallow a donkey and its cart. Arriving at a river, the MRAPs lumber down a dirt trail to the dry wadi. As the development team's MRAP lurches across the graveled riverbed, I look up at the rusting steel bridge overhead. The commander says, "We try not to use bridges. IEDs." He pauses. "And we're not so sure they can handle the weight."

The bad road is the least of our problems. "That's where that IED was," the security sergeant says as we pass a clot of kids, a flash of red, yellow, and gray, their scowling eyes following us. It's a desolate area, worn-out mountains to the south, a trickle of a brown river running beside barren escarpments. "We try to keep our eyes out," a grunt says. "You never know, small arms, IEDs, freshly dug spots." Before we left, the gunner quizzed me. "I'm on the .240. Ammo's there in the boxes," pointing to the metal boxes stacked beside my seat. "You pass them up if I need it?"

USAID and the development lobby sold the road as the great insurgency killer, the old "development yields security" ploy. The oft-repeated slogan was "The insurgency ends where the road begins." Wouldn't it be lovely to think so? When I ask one officer what he thinks, he snorts, "The insurgency doesn't end at the road, that's where it begins." The Ring Road became a Taliban magnet, the place where they emplaced IEDs, mounted ambushes, and set up money-spinning checkpoints. And here we are, a decade after the road reconstruction, needing a full security platoon buttoned up in MRAPs to go twenty miles from one fort to another. We pass unit after unit of Romanian soldiers out on anti-IED patrols, cautiously peering into culverts, sweeping with their mine detectors. Long lines of convoys of MRAPs from decommissioned US bases retrograde toward Kabul as the Taliban take over the districts they are leaving. Roads brings security—yeah, right.

⋮   ⋮   ⋮   ⋮   ⋮

The development team is on a WHAM mission. They want to talk to some Afghans who are building a *karez*, Afghanistan's ancient irrigation system of underground channels that carries mountain water to the fields with minimal evaporation.

In the twilight of the counterinsurgency (and aid funding), US development solons are suddenly deciding it might be best to let the Afghans do it the Afghan way. The official word is filtering down to

the development units: let Haji do it like his granddad did. Grape growing is another example. The Afghans have been growing grapes for centuries, quite well, actually. For generations, Afghanistan was a major
raisin exporter. Farmers in Afghanistan traditionally grew their vines
on low earthen mounds. But for years and years, USAID and the USDA
insisted the Afghans needed to trellis their grapes. It was the go-to agricultural project for US development teams and their "implementing
partners," aka beltway bandits. "They just let their vines lay on the
ground," development officials would tsk as they touted their grand (and
profitable) trellising projects. But as it turned out, the Afghan way of
letting the vines grow on low mounds worked better in their harsh, desiccating environment. "Last six-eight months, they're telling us, better
keep the vines on the ground; dries out less," the commander tells me.
"Another example that the Afghan way is the best way." If only they'd
known before dozens and dozens of development contractors launched
hundreds, maybe thousands of worthless trellising projects across Afghanistan. But how else will an American development professional pay
for the kids' private schools? The Lexus?

And almost since the Americans invaded, they've been digging
wells in Afghanistan. Thousands and thousands of wells. What could
be nicer? Give a village a well. And more importantly, give a nice profitable contract to a development corporation. A former water resources
development adviser to the United States, NATO, and the Kabul government tells me about the pressure to let contracts without forethought or
oversight: "The drumbeat was 'We've got to spend money, and we're going
to spend!'"

She's a clear-eyed Midwesterner who'd hitched her star to the science
of hydrology. After earning degrees from one of America's top universities,
she worked for many years as an environmental consultant, investigating
and cleaning up hazardous-waste sites in the Pacific Northwest. She knew
science and she knew water, and she knew what happened when things
went wrong.

She went out to Afghanistan as a civilian member of the Army Corps
of Engineers. Military civil affairs officers had told me years before about
this straight-shooting woman hydrologist, who was trying to stop some
of the worst USAID and beltway-bandit dams and wells, like some sort of

Cassandra of Afghan water projects. The officers thought she was right. They thought she was cool. The hydrologist thought she could do some good, but in her years of trying, she learned otherwise. "If the American people really knew how much money has been wasted," the hydrologist says. "It's appalling. . . . It's grim."

Beyond the waste of American taxpayer money, what is the problem with wells? Well, there are a lot of problems: Out in the countryside, powerful Afghans grab control of the precious water, creating unforeseen tribal tensions. The essentially uncoordinated well-digging frenzy disrupts the fragile, semiarid ecosystem. "Westerners come in and think groundwater will be replenished, but that is not the case in Afghanistan," the hydrologist tells me. As water tables drop, previously fertile fields are rendered unusable. "Here I was, this water advocate, and I was saying: 'Stop!'" The negative impact is apparent within a few years, but even as poorly built tube wells collapse and water tables plummet, USAID is contracting with the beltway bandit ARD (Association for Rural Development) to drill ten thousand wells. The contract name: "Sustainable Water Supply and Sanitation." It would be funny, if it weren't so tragic.

In booming Kabul, US-financed wells tapped a finite aquifer of twenty-thousand-year-old water, which the refugees and opportunists thronging the city are rapidly draining. "There's a lot of drama in the water sector," the hydrologist says. "Kabul is in dire straits. In a sense, they are mining their water. Kabul's going to run out of water." Disillusioned by the waste and failed policies, the highly credentialed and highly respected hydrologist quit in disgust. She is getting a degree in nursing.

So with the US aid spigot turning off, the development consultants are not unexpectedly touting traditional Afghan karez systems. The aid money for wells and dams is drying up anyway. And so, rolling down Route One in our armored convoy, we are trying to find some Afghan karez workers. High on a hillside above the highway, we see Afghans beside a wooden windlass. We pull to the side of the road. The grunts clamber out first to establish a security perimeter. Hand signals and we begin climbing the steep slope. "Walk in my footsteps," one of the grunts instructs me. "Mines." Watching where he goes.

As we talk to the two karez workers, I feel like I am in profound Afghanistan; real Afghanistan. The Afghanistan where laborers make a dollar or two for a day's work. A long, long way from the sleek technocrats of Kabul, the plump government officials, the well-paid interpreters, the oily contractors with their hands out. These are tiny, malnourished men with large hungry eyes. Reminds me that Afghanistan has one of the lowest caloric intakes in the world; farm families slowly starving through much of the winter. I look around the stark landscape and wonder how anyone can wrest a living from this. The men are digging a new karez for an Afghan police commander. They are using a battered old wooden windlass called a *sarkh* to haul the dirt out of the small hole that plummets black into the earth. The sarkh looks like something out of the bible: two wooden Xs on an axle with angled stepping boards so the men can use leg power to haul up the dirt. The men stop to speak with us, seemingly nonplussed by heavily armed foreigners dressed like storm troopers. One brushes back his long black hair from his eyes and tells us they first used a pickaxe and shovel to dig a pit about two feet by three feet and thirty feet deep. Then they set up their sarkh and began tunneling. A muffled call drifts up from the hole, and I realize with a start that there is a laboring man far down that shaft. They jump to the sarkh and a yellow plastic bucket eventually emerges from the abyss. They'd been working for two months and thought they'd work another six months. The commander admires their foot-powered sarkh, says it is way better than the tripod and hand-crank system the now karez-crazy Americans are giving to villagers. Lord only knows what the development companies charge the American taxpayers for those shiny metal contraptions.

The worker steps from the sarkh, brushes his hank of hair back again, and tells us they have no education, so they can't get good government jobs. He says he is supporting his family of twelve or thirteen. None of his younger five brothers can afford an education, so they will also be doing manual labor. Unblinking, he keeps staring at us. Another muffled call from the shaft, and the Afghan returns to the windlass.

FOURTEEN

Friends

MOHAMMAD AHMED AND AMINALLA ARE FARMERS, BUT VERY special farmers: government farmers. The father and grown son work on the Zabul Province government demonstration farm that the Americans built. It's great job. Nice place. Walls. Security guards. High pay, and the Americans cough up amazing amounts of stuff that can be skimmed. But as they talk to the American commander, they are petulant. Mohammad Ahmed and Aminalla want something, and can't believe the Americans aren't hopping to it.

Back in Washington, President Hamid Karzai is having the same problem. Karzai flew to DC with a shopping list for his American friends. The night before, in the FOB's small plywood rec center, I watched MSNBC commentators parse the Karzai-Obama chess game. Big-screen TV high on the wall amid shelves of DVDs and dog-eared paperbacks. The frantic click of dominos from a fervid game going on beneath the talking heads. Clickclickclickclickclickclick. Grunts with their eyes fixed on the board, bantering quietly. The eminences exchanged their spins: Secretary of State Hillary Clinton wants fifteen thousand troops post-2014; President Obama wants only the bare minimum, maybe three thousand. The Pentagon always wants more. Other spokespeople float out the zero option: no troops. Karzai wants wants wants. Can't blame Karzai for expecting to get his way. For a dozen years the Americans always caved. Couldn't look weak before the elections; had to punch their ticket for the CV; one more rotation for retirement; just give the Afghans what they want. Talking heads conjecture about multiyear commitments on US troops, air assets, helicopters, money, lots and lots of money. The grunts don't even look up. Clickclickclickclickclickclick.

Standing in a field at the demo farm, Mohammad Ahmed and Aminalla want a new fence. The Americans paid for other fences. Why not this one? There is clearly some Afghan denial going on. The Afghans have watched the retrograde convoys motoring down Route One, but they simply can't imagine a country rich enough, or foolish enough, to just walk away from the enormous investment poured into Afghanistan. Just can't imagine it. The Afghans know the game will be up if the Americans leave. Some anger is simmering. One US combat commander told me his Afghan army counterpart flared up when he learned that American support was being scaled back. It was edgy, the commander said. How long before the Afghan anger erupts into violence against the retreating Americans?

Bearded, turbaned, intent, Mohammad Ahmed keeps waving his arm toward the far end of the farm. There, they need a fence there. Sometimes goats get in. Another nice fat fence project. As he waves his arm, his bright gold wristwatch flashes in the high sun. An officer standing beside me mutters that the farmer's gold watch signifies extraordinary wealth—and sometimes Taliban ties. The commander tells Mohammad Ahmed that his team isn't doing projects anymore. He should ask his provincial agriculture minister to build the fence. The son scowls and looks away. Mohammad Ahmed steps away and glares.

The commander points to a small, open, concrete shed with a tin roof that stands out on the small road in front of the demo farm. "Farm Collection Point," he scoffs. "USAID—$40,000 each." Some bright American development consultant came up with the idea that all the Afghan farmers in the area could bring their produce to a central location, where traders would come to get the lot. "Total bust," the commander says, telling me that the collection points failed for multiple reasons. "Well, first, the farmers didn't want to mix their produce together. And then most of the collection points were way off the beaten path." Even this one is pretty far off Route One. "We found one that was in the middle of nowhere. Nowhere. It wasn't on a road, not even on an *unpaved* road." And to top it all off, the tin roofs essentially cooked the produce. Given the insecurity, lousy locations, and wilted produce, it isn't surprising to learn that the traders never came to USAID's collection points. The commander says Afghans stripped most of the tin roofs off almost immediately after construction. He tells me, "The only reason that one still has its tin roof is because it's right next to the demo farm."

Mohammad Ahmed and Aminalla regroup and return for another round. Forced smiles. The Americans need to contract for the fence. The Americans already built all these fences. All these buildings. They need to build the fence. "We don't do projects anymore," the commander patiently repeats. "Ask the DAIL, the agriculture director, to do it. Put it in his budget to send to the MAIL [Ministry of Agriculture, Irrigation, and Livestock] in Kabul for the money. Ask the DAIL to do it." Mohammad Ahmed retorts that the ministry is "weak," so the American "friends" need to do it. Smiles fading as the commander again says, "We don't do projects anymore. Talk to your DAIL." Disgruntled, the father and son stand together as the security soldiers vector back from their perimeter. "Let them go first," a grunt says to me as two Afghan policemen come out of a building. "We don't trust them." The commander says good-bye to Mohammad Ahmed and Aminalla, and we head for the convoy.

FIFTEEN

Kandahar

THE PORTLY CONTRACTOR WOLFS HIS FOOD AT THE KANDAHAR DFAC, a dining facility that resembles a wealthy suburban high school cafeteria. Perky super-graphics line the walls. Grumpy workers in white uniforms at the bewildering array of steam tables, grills, and food bars serve far too many food choices—American, Mexican, Indian, Oriental, fried, fresh; desserts at the special food bar; a designated breakfast cereal counter; a state-of-the-art, serve-yourself espresso and cappuccino maker.

Cliques of unfathomable specificity and complexity people the long lines of Formica tables. US officers there, grunts there, further divided by units and specialties. Contractors in clots.

The fleshy contractor is flush-faced, with a graying goatee. He scrapes his pasteboard plate with his plastic fork so enthusiastically I think he might tunnel through. He has the full spec ops going-to-war costume: 5.11 tactical pants with a dozen pockets, a khaki back-to-Africa bwana shirt, and a floppy flat-crowned field hat that hangs on a cord down his back. So new, the clothes still have creases. He's a haw haw haw kind of guy. As he scarfs down his food, he joshes with the stoic Slovakian sitting beside him. The contractor jokes at length about French military ineptitude: "Who had to bail 'em out in both world wars? Us!" Haw haw haw! The slender Slovakian murmurs something. The contractor shovels in a big mouthful and talks as he chews. "But, you know, the French, they gave all these great gifts to the world," and he leans toward the Slovak. "They have all their great cheese," and whisper, whisper, whisper. Haw haw haw! The Slovak smiles wanly. A couple more mouthfuls of food and the contractor abruptly changes subjects: "You know, we're in draw-down." The Slovak agrees warily. The contractor bellows his punch line: "We got to keep this military machine going—so we can all make money!" Haw haw haw!

: : : : :

KAF (Kandahar Air Field) is the logistics and transshipment center for US-led coalition operations in southeastern Afghanistan. My public affairs handler is a short, dark sergeant who says, "Aloha." She's part of a resolutely Hawaiian team of National Guard soldiers who run the KAF public affairs office. Even their e-mails begin with "Aloha!" Beside their media center, the islanders have a thatched beach palapa hung with a Hawaiian flag for their smoke breaks, with island music softly playing from the speakers. But like all the public affairs officers, they stick to the victory narrative. It's hard-core information operations: everything is A-OK in KAF. They churn out the bullshit and I write it down, thinking what the fuck? Do they really believe this? But they know the real story. On a bulletin board, a red, white, and blue poster of a saluting blond 1940s-era woman typist reads, "YOU WRITE WHAT YOU'RE TOLD!" At the bottom, the copy reads, "THANKS CORPORATE NEWS! We couldn't control the people without you! A message from the Department of Homeland Security."

As I walk down the halls or across the base, the real story comes out, often in sotto voce shorthand and code. "Look at this website," soldiers mutter as they pass me a piece of paper. A contractor quietly suggests, "Have you asked about that?" Press relations and happy talk isn't masking the increasing insecurity and growing cynicism. It's adding to it.

The PAOs give me a bunk for the night and precise instructions what to do if the Giant Voice announces an attack. The sergeant shows me the nearest concrete bunker. At 2:15 a.m., the base's sirens begin whooping and the Giant Voice blares an unintelligible warning—something, something, "attack." Per directives, I hit the ground for two minutes. Wrestling my boots on, I hurry to the bunker nearest the media center. It's empty. Where is everybody? I wander back to bed. The next morning I ask a sergeant about the alert. "False alarm," he says. I tell him I couldn't understand the message. "British voice," he replies with a smile. KAF is a NATO base, so the allies negotiated alternating voices on the Giant Voice. Sure enough, a few hours later I'm working in my room when the whoop-whoopwhoop starts up again, and a woman's mash-up British accent begins repeating, "Grawn at tak grawn at tak." More whoops, then a plummy male voice, perhaps Kiwi BBC, intones, "This is a test of 'Ground Attack.'" I get up off the floor. An electronic warble, then the woman, "Awwwl clee-ah," wailing sirens, then just the sound of desert wind, rotors, and departing warplanes.

: : : : :

With the retrograde going full bore, Kandahar Air Field is overflowing with transiting soldiers and contractors, who are jammed into the barrios of "tin-can" metal housing pods and Alaska tents. More are coming. One of the PA sergeants tells me, "It's going to get bigger before it gets smaller," and wonders where they are going to stack the soldiers, because they sure aren't breaking the wire in Kandahar, no sir.

In the evening, the soldiers and contractors throng the KAF board-walk, a carnivalesque piece of America dropped into central Asia. With a covered wooden walkway and glass-fronted emporiums, it's the Jersey Shore and a mid-America shopping mall tackily reproduced in southern Afghanistan. The half-mile-square quadrangle boasts three dozen glass-fronted emporiums, including a TGI Fridays ("In here, it's always Friday"), a KFC, a Tim Horton's, a pizza place, a French bakery, a Green Beans coffee shop ("Honor First, Coffee Second"), Indian fast food, Afghan kabobs, a shawarma shop, an ice cream parlor, a book store, an ATM, an internet café, a barber shop, and souvenir stores. It's a polder of concentrated American-ness surrounded by otherness, an otherness that can only be negotiated in armored vehicles and fast-moving aircraft, an unfathomable otherness that triggers an existential fear only suppressed with bright lights and signifiers of home. One night, as a cold dusty wind blows in from the desert, I buy a hot dog at Nathan's. "All food from America," the sign promises. The bun is stale.

The boardwalk surrounds a large illuminated field with an Astroturfed soccer field, a volleyball court, a basketball court, and a concrete field hockey rink for the Canadian troops. Runners in electric colors jog by. A trio of elderly be-turbaned Afghan men plod from garbage can to garbage can, looking around anxiously as they empty each container. A solitary soldier strides across the field, his weapon across his chest, barrel down. Twinkle lights sparkle on the storefronts and boardwalk. Neon signs cast a lovely glow. Romantic, except the Taliban is right over there. Occasionally, right here. Luckily, for that, there is the Deutscher PX, a kind of Cabela's big-box sporting goods store for men whose quarry is other men. Deutscher Service PX ("Military Supply. Worldwide. Kosovo Afghanistan") purveys upscale Bad Boy toys: tactical and survival knives, sniper scopes, Glocks, Heckler & Kochs, and other warfare bric-a-brac—ballistic protection, $400 Oakley sunglasses, holsters and tac bags, carabineers, tactical clothes (the contractor's new clothes?), camelback canteens, and the like. The store is crammed with soldiers and civilians. Tall spec ops soldiers tower above the other soldiers and pudgy contractors. Rail-thin Indian contractors stare aghast at the prices.

A couple of British officers are chortling as they pass Duetscher PX. One smirks as he reports that the boardwalk businesses are contributing $125,000 to $150,000 each month "to the war effort." Sucking soldiers dry is big business here. Haw haw haw.

It all reminds me of First Lieutenant Milo Minderbinder, the proto–war entrepreneur of Joseph Heller's *Catch-22* who coolly said, "I didn't start this war, Yossarian. I'm just trying to put it on a business-like basis. Is there anything wrong with that?"

: : : : :

I walk through the boardwalk on my way to Kandahar Air Field's legendary landmark: the Poo Pond, a lake-sized pool of human excrement that shimmers in the middle of KAF's barracks and offices. Does it smell? Oh, yes. It smells, eye-watering smelly, nose-running smelly. "You've got to see it," soldiers told me. "Just follow your nose." Constructed in the first years of the war, the Poo Pond became the stuff of legend when rumors began circulating that a spec ops soldier swam across the sea of poop to win a bet. When a journalist quizzed US Special Operations Command about the rumor, the SOCOM spokesperson refused to confirm or deny the story, giving black ops a whole new meaning in Kandahar.

I arrive at the pond, which is about a hundred yards wide with a festive fountain spurting brown water in the middle. A warning sign is posted lakeside: "Biohazard. Do Not Enter," as though the sharp tang of twenty thousand people's sewage is not enough to dissuade me from a dip. I am digging into a story: Just before I left for Afghanistan, an air force officer contacted me with a dirty secret: The Poo Pond is financing the Taliban. As the officer explained it, the military, having failed to build a replacement wastewater plant in 2009 because the Afghan contracting company went belly up, decided they needed to de-sludge the sewage lagoon. That part came out OK. The de-sludging contractor dredged almost two million gallons of sludge out the pond, and then mixed it with solids. After it was dried, the mix was great topsoil, nontoxic and not even smelly because of the exposure to air and sun. According to the officer, this is where it got nasty. He and others thought the concentrated sludge should be given or sold to impoverished Afghan farmers as organic fertilizer. Concentrated sludge has been sold as fertilizer in the United States since the 1920s. But instead of enriching Afghan soil, the US-led coalition forces decided to burn the mountains of fertilizer with astronomically expensive imported gasoline. The officer reminded me that the Taliban got $1,500 in protection money for each US fuel tanker they let through, so in the process the jihadists were also able to skim the American shit.

Walking back, I spot a green metal dumpster stenciled with a large sign that reads, "General Waste Only." At that moment, it seems to sum up the whole war.

SIXTEEN

Leatherneck

THE TALIBAN HEARTLAND OF HELMAND IS THE WORST, soldiers tell me, rolling their eyes and saying "Good luck" when they learn where I am headed. One ruefully laughs, "Hope your insurance is paid up." A photojournalist tells me my embed area is called the "Heart of Darkness" for its unending attacks.

It's a long, cold January journey from Kandahar to Camp Leatherneck, not even a hundred miles away. When we board the C-17 cargo plane that night, it is already heavily loaded with pallets, so we shuffle sideways with our packs to get to the seats. There's a long wait, then a forklift loads two more giant pallets full of rocket pods. "Marines got to have more rockets," a chaplain says. Too many rockets—the plane is now tail heavy. So we wait for hours in the open plane while they reconfigure the load. It's 4:45 in the morning when I finally gimp down the C-17's aluminum ramp in Helmand.

I've landed in a thirty-six-square-mile military redoubt that includes the Brits' Camp Bastion airfield, where Prince Harry famously served; the ANA's Camp Shorabak, and Camp Leatherneck, the largest marine base in Afghanistan. When US forces surged in 2009, the marines took over the battle in Helmand. Camp Leatherneck became the feudal capital of Marineistan, where the victory narrative is still being bellowed with a full-throated roar—despite the receding surge and the Taliban's resilient strength.

I am wary of my Marineistan reception. The marines had jerked around my Helmand embed requests for months, approving and canceling in a maddening roundelay. At one point, the lead marine public affairs officer questioned my *Foreign Policy* article, "The Juice Ain't Worth the Squeeze," which was critical of the botched counterinsurgency. "Is this you?" the PAO testily asked. Yep, it's me. He'd recently written an eyebrow-raising article that claimed the US-led coalition was "winning the war," so I offered to discuss our perspectives when I was at Leatherneck. That generated yet another embed cancelation.

But here I am at Camp Leatherneck, freezing and exhausted and hoping for the best. My PAO contact arrives, a marine lieutenant who's fit, alert, and informed, with a flawless hair bun that belies the early hour. She tells me the marines have arranged for me to hitch a helicopter ride with a commander who is flying to the Helmand Valley forward operating base where I am embedding. The Osprey flight leaves early in the morning. In the meantime, I need heat; I need sleep.

Soon she is dropping me at a large bedraggled tent in a warren of woebegone canvas hooches. When I enter the tent, I quickly realize I am the only one there. Dozens of bunks are empty. The roaring furnace fan promises warmth, until I realize it is blasting cold air. It's an icehouse. I'm shivering as I race to put on extra clothes, get into my sleeping bag, and set an alarm before I conk out.

A frigid, gray dawn is leaching over the tents when I emerge semi-frozen and stiff a few hours later. Stumbling down the walkways, I figure out the tents are for Third World workers who do the base's grunt work. Cheery Indians point me to the blessedly warm DFAC, where I binge on sugar-fortified coffee and extraordinary amounts of carbs.

The lieutenant is smirking when she picks me up for the Osprey ride, though she lightens up when I don't grouse about the cold. On the way to the landing zone, she tells me she's an Annapolis grad. It's obvious she's an extremely competent soldier, one of those young Americans whom anyone would be proud to have as a son or daughter. Despite my efforts to tidy up, I am at best disheveled, in contrast to the lieutenant, who is crisp and together. I confess to being amazed by the female marines' perfect hair buns. How do they do that? And she tells me their secret for preternaturally tight and immaculate hair buns: lots of hair gel and a sock bun or two to keep it all together. "Yeah, we kind of look down on those sloppy hair buns the army females have," she says with marine pride.

She's also a marine officer who sticks to the talking points. We began talking about the fifteen Taliban fighters who recently stormed the camp, killing two marines and destroying six marine jets valued at over $200 million—the largest loss of marine aircraft since the Vietnam War. Soldiers had already confided to me that the base's perimeter defenses were a joke, little more than razor wire in many places. Insurgents could walk onto the base. They said that prior to the attack, the arrogant marine commander had reduced patrols and assigned perimeter security to unreliable Pacific Islanders. In the face of the almost unfathomable defeat, the lieutenant is bright, upbeat, focusing on what she calls the "hero stories." She's clearly going places in the hierarchy.

⋮   ⋮   ⋮   ⋮   ⋮

Leatherneck seems rife with self-delusional victory spiels and the psychological twistings of the traumatized. The marines thought themselves indomitable when they rolled into dry, dusty Helmand, but hardscrabble Afghans armed with farm-fertilizer bombs, old Soviet weapons, and spray cans taped with cigarette lighters had thwarted them. Now they have an unhealthy love-hate fixation with the place. "The marines spilled blood here," one consultant tells me. "They can't let it go."

The marines invaded a counterinsurgency nightmare: a predatory Afghan government; a popularly supported Taliban controlling broad swaths of the province. The surge's massive military offensives provided only brief respites before the insurgency lit things up again with thousands of kinetic attacks. IEDs and ambushes were so common that marines patrolled with a tourniquet on each limb, ready to be tightened when they got hit. US military hospitals were filled with marine amputees—double amputees, triple amputees, quadruple amputees. Congressman Walter Jones, an anti–Afghanistan War Republican from North Carolina whose district includes the sprawling Camp Lejeune marine base, told me of visiting a constituent in Walter Reed Hospital. "Douglas," he told me, "there was nothing below his waist, nothing. There was nothing but *air*." Yeah, the marines spilled a lot of blood in Helmand Province.

Official pronunciamentos about "winning the war" aside, the marines know they are leaving soon. Most jarheads still on the ground
don't believe in the failed counterinsurgency mission. They are just trying to stay alive.

And the marine command sure knows they are going. With all
the retrograded military gear flooding into the base, the command had
to expand the Camp Leatherneck scrap yard. "They've taken up that
whole square now," one soldier tells me as we drive past an enormous
compound.

Names tell stories: the compound used to known as the DRMO, Defense Reutilization and Marketing Office, a vast recycling yard filled
with almost good-as-new military equipment. But as the marines turned
their thoughts to going, the compound got a new name: Defense Logistics Agency Disposition Services, with the emphasis on disposing. The
scrap yard is a din of hissing cutting torches and the grinding of Big Red,
the shredder that devours everything, including concertina wire, Hesco
barriers, MRAPs, and gargantuan armored anti-IED vehicles. It all becomes scrap metal, so the equipment doesn't fall into the hands of the
Taliban. Rebutting the victory narrative, the scrapped military equipment serves as an obvious no-confidence vote.

And like an estranged, soon-to-be-gone spouse, the marine command doesn't even want to occupy their new house. At the height of the
spare-no-cost surge, the appropriations-flush military contracted for a
lavish $34 million, sixty-four-thousand-square-foot command center to
be built at Leatherneck. The marines never even moved in. Soldiers
laughingly point it out, a vast, empty, white elephant that hulks a short
walking distance from the plywood buildings of the marine command
headquarters.

One day I am walking across the command compound with a group
of officers and contractors. As we pass the flagpole that designates the commanding general's headquarters, I see a large tom turkey skulking beside
the building. Before I can even ask, the turkey comes running toward us
with an outstretched neck and an angry look. "Eh, he's been cranky since
his hen died," one officer says. "He just skulks around and pecks the soldiers. The general is concerned. Wants us to get him another hen."

I'm thinking someone is going to burst out laughing, but no, the group is dead serious. They talk about the challenges of getting a healthy replacement hen to Camp Leatherneck to assuage Tom's frustration. Hyena got his first hen. Second one was sickly and died. Someone mentions that USAID's got an agricultural development project with turkeys in Lashkar Gah, the nearby provincial capital. Some good hens there. I can see hope in the warriors' eyes. Ever resourceful, they discuss the dangers of an overland turkey mission. Too risky. Send a helicopter for the bird, they decide. That's the answer.

SEVENTEEN

Sex

AFGHANISTAN IS A PRUDE'S WAR IN SOME WAYS. IT'S A CON-
servative Islamic country, so soldiers are prohibited from drinking
alcohol. The random military substance-abuse tests discourage drug use,
even in this country awash with dope. The soldiers' main opiates are
big-screen ESPN and video games. Carousing with the locals ain't happening: the soldiers are penned up, very seldom "breaking the wire"
(leaving the base); 90 percent never do. The Afghanistan War's R&R is
definitely no Bangkok bacchanal. It's a four-day pass to the US base in
Qatar, highlighted by three military-supervised beers and boneless
chicken wings at Chili's. With the retrograde, soldiers now have to
take R&R on their Afghanistan bases—"Freedom Rest," some flack
named it.

But soldiers are soldiers, and sex is a grand distraction, whether
it's the Leatherneck general's turkey concerns, General Petraeus's dalli-
ances with Paula Broadwell, or Commanding General John Allen's flirta-
tious e-mails to socialite Jill Kelley. And lord knows the troops do their
best under the circumstances. Like the hypersexed Olympic villages, the
bases are full of extremely fit, adrenaline-pumped young people who
figure out how to get it done. Frontline attractions are consummated in
blast bunkers, empty plywood B-huts, and Porta Potties—"If that Porta
Potty is rocking . . ."

There are frantic hookups, momentary diversions from the awful
reality. One burly specialist tells me with a quaking voice that an affair
in Iraq almost cost him his marriage. Took a lot of counseling when he
got home to work things out. "We're going to make it," he says with a

relieved smile. Six harrowing months into his rotation in Afghanistan, he's hooked up again. "War scares me," he says with downcast eyes. "It does."

Then there are the romances that bloom in the war zone, like flowers emerging from shattered concrete. I watch as two young officers shyly bond, the furtive handholding, the whispered wedding plans, the commanding officer's obvious efforts to avoid noticing the forbidden relationship. Love on the battlefield.

And yes, the soldiers get it done, to the point that pregnancy is the number one reason for emergency evacuation of female soldiers, who make up about 20 percent of US forces in Afghanistan. And that is despite the rapidly depleted racks of condoms that hang in every front-line PX. Filled to the brim with rubbers one day, *gone* the next. I think, when do they find time? One NATO soldier, who didn't know she was pregnant, even gave birth at Camp Bastion in Helmand.

With the shortage of women, it's a sellers' market. Soldiers and contractors joke about "mission-pretty" women and coyotes' hunting preserves. It brings out a surreal war-zone sexuality: a short, stocky, middle-aged contractor with a mule face and a sultry honey-blond Veronica Lake hairdo; an almost pathologically muscular man over-pumped with supplements and far too many hours in the gym with fetishistic fitness regimes. More than once I hear women say, "The odds are good, but the goods are odd."

And being the war, there is commerce. One night at Camp Leatherneck, a plump young woman says "Hi!" to a major and me as we approach our sleeping quarters in a lineup of prefab metal "cans." He warily responds as we walk past. Normally a friendly guy, I'm surprised at his response. "She's a contractor," he laughs. "Works at the base post office. I see her out here a lot. I think she moonlights." Sure enough, there she is the next night, trolling between the blast barriers and the latrines. Last I see her, she's heading for a can with a young marine.

Sex is a weapon in this battle for hearts and minds: CIA agents handing out Viagra to elderly Afghan tribal leaders with multiple wives, claiming the little blue pills stiffen anti-Taliban resistance when the chieftains return to "an authoritative position." DynCorp contractors pleasing warlords with tarted-up boy prostitutes at *bacha-bazi* ("playing

with boys") parties. A Texas NGO, Comfort Aid International, funding
dowries and weddings in Helmand so sexually frustrated young Afghan
men don't join the Taliban in quest of the martyrs' reward of seventy-two
celestial virgins.

Sexual assaults on the military bases are the dirty secret of the post-
9/11 wars. The VA reported that 15 percent of female patients who are
Iraq and Afghanistan veterans screened positive for military sexual
trauma. On one forward operating base in eastern Afghanistan, I can see
the pattern in color: Because of attacks, the FOB is blacked out at night,
requiring male soldiers to negotiate the base with red-, blue-, and green-
lensed flashlights. Leaving a lighted building, night-blindness presents
an unsetting vulnerability till your eyes adjust. Because female soldiers
are so often groped when leaving the latrines, they are permitted to use
white lights, giving the pitch-black base a flickering firefly-like color-
coded gender ID system.

Sexual harassment combines with this 360-degree war's combat
stress. Women face the same rockets, IEDs, and ambushes as men, as well
as equivalent rates of PTSD (post-traumatic stress disorder). It's equal-
opportunity danger that belies the Pentagon policy officially banning
women from combat roles. A female colonel says to me after leading
a mission into Taliban territory, "This policy makes no sense. We go
through the same training as men, know how to use the same weapons,
carry the same loads in the field. We face the same threats."

Women learn how to cope. One day I'm strapped into an MRAP on
a mission with a team of security grunts and a tall, blond medic. Raised
on a farm in upstate New York, she's a mother. Reaches across the cabin
to show me a picture of her toddler daughter at home with her family.
Joined the National Guard to help with college tuition. Now she's in
an armored gun truck in dangerous country, with a squad of nervous
soldiers who are rattling the intercom with typical truck banter, their
chatter about TV, movies, and food abruptly veering into very graphic
locker-room sex bluster—no hole unexplored. The over-testosteroned
braggadocio is making me uncomfortable for the woman, but she never
flinches. As the bonehead blather reaches a climax, she keys her micro-
phone, and begins describing her daughter's birth, explicitly recounting
the long labor, the racking contractions, the gushing fluids. She revels in

the gore, grinning as she describes bloody slop and torn tissue. "You want to talk sex, boys," she seems to be saying, "Let's talk sex." The acne-scarred grunts are now crimson; intent on their views out the bulletproof glass. One soldier heckles half-heartedly, but she persists to the end of her story: "So the doctor gave me the scalpel and asked, 'Did I want to cut the cord?'" There is dead silence on the intercom. She smiles at me and pats her blond hair bun.

EIGHTEEN

Drugs

THE CONVOY LUMBERS ACROSS THE MOONSCAPE OF THE
central Helmand River valley, the epicenter of America's futile efforts to
remake Afghanistan in its own image. Generations of American developers have come to this austere landscape intent on transforming it into the
breadbasket of Afghanistan and a bastion of democratic values. Instead,
they created the world's largest opium poppy plantation.

Kid Rock is playing on the MRAP intercom as we judder down a
rocky track snaking through the rolling tan desert, heading to Nawa.
"Stay to the right there," the navigator points. "IEDs." Veering right, the
gun truck driver manages to use "fuck" as a verb, adverb, adjective, and
noun in the same sentence. We follow the massive anti-IED mine roller
through the fine khaki dust. A cloud enshrouds us; visibility drops to
a few feet. A boil of yellow smears the horizon as we approach a low mud
village. Beside their ragged tents, nomadic Kuchis with hard faces stare
as we pass. A turbaned man on a tiny trotting donkey glares. An insouci-
ant camel masticates. A flock of fat-tailed sheep waggle by.

There is suddenly a sparkle of water coursing down a narrow canal,
watering a small field of straggly cotton plants. "Cotton, for oil and meal,"
the major says over the intercom. "Alternative Livelihood." The canal is
part of the great Helmand-Arghandab Valley Authority (HAVA) irrigation system, the pride of the ambitious Cold War–era agronomists and
engineers who came in the 1950s to make the southern Afghanistan
desert bloom with the gargantuan Kajaki Dam and a vast system of
waterways. Calling their headquarter town at Lashkar Gah "Little America," they were confident there wasn't a thing that could go wrong. With

its dams, canals, hydroelectric power, and new colonies of resettled Pashtuns, it was going to be the Hoover Dam and Imperial Valley in Afghanistan; a capitalist riposte to the Soviet Union's equally ambitious development projects in the north. It was Cold War big-think. And of course it all went to hell.

The gigantic project sucked up goat-choking amounts of money. Each year the salaries for the American engineers and consultants alone cost the equivalent of Afghanistan's total exports. The lack of land titles forced most of the resettled Pashtuns into tenant farming. The canals soon silted up. The reservoirs raised the water table, which leached salts and gypsum to the surface, desiccating vineyards and orchards.

But we are talking about pride (and development contracts) here, so the United States kept the HAVA irrigation and hydroelectric systems going through the 1960s and 1970s, making Helmand the country's most productive region for cotton and grain. But after the Soviet invasion in 1979, the United States pulled the plug on HAVA. As anarchy spread during the 1980s US-supported mujahideen war against the Soviets, opium poppy began to replace cotton and grain, facilitated by the CIA to finance the jihadi warlords' fight against the communists. By the 1990s civil war, the US-financed Helmand River valley irrigation system was watering the world's largest opium poppy region. There were poppy fields to the horizon. This wasn't just small-scale dirt farming. This was tractor-powered agribusiness, with elaborate credit, refining, and distribution arrangements—until the Taliban government outlawed opium poppy production in 2000, after decreeing it un-Islamic. On the eve of 9/11, Afghan poppy production fell almost to zero.

And then America invaded. Hungry for targets, the United States bombed the Kajaki Dam in 2001. And then quickly gave lucrative reconstruction contracts to beltway bandit Louis Berger Group to rebuild it. The Washington way: build it, blow it up, rebuild it—everybody makes money.

After the Taliban government fell, opium poppy production in Helmand soared, most often controlled by American-allied Afghan drug lords, who naturally also maintained their connections to the Taliban. So, everybody got a share. By 2004, almost 90 percent of the world's illicit opium was coming from Afghanistan, abetted by a US counternarcotics strategy that was bipolar to the extreme. The US command repeatedly unleashed offensives to retake control of the major Helmand opium centers, but ordered their soldiers to ignore the poppy fields to avoid disrupting the Afghan farmers' major cash crop. "Per command, we don't talk about poppy," the major says. A civilian ag contractor chimes in, "The dirty word: 'poppy.' In ten months, I haven't seen a poppy—officially."

To ostensibly win the farmers' hearts and minds, the US development agencies launched lavishly funded "Alternative Livelihood" programs to replace poppy with other crops—billions of dollars spent to reduce poppy cultivation. The major simply says, "We offer alternatives." After the last big marine offensive in 2010, USAID threw about $30 million at Nawa's seventy-five thousand inhabitants over nine months—$400 for every man, woman, and child in a country where the annual per capita income is only $400 a year. Some called it "carpet bombing Nawa with money."

It was the standard WHAM lineup of absurdly expensive development contracts for the beltway bandits: projects to encourage cultivation of pie-in-the-sky alternative crops like saffron; cash-for-work schemes to give fighters a handout until the next ambush; unsustainable construction projects. The major laughs about "that big IRD [International Relief and Development] project in Nawa": millions for solar panels to power streetlights and electricity for the bazaar. But IRD failed to procure the batteries the system required. "By the time they arrived, the system was outdated," he chuckles. "Great idea but poor execution."

It's all a giant, expensive bust. As we trundle toward Nawa, the UN Office on Drugs and Crime is reporting record Afghan poppy harvests from dramatically increased cultivation, the Afghan government is increasingly corrupt, and the Taliban is stronger than ever. "IED crater," the major says as we pass a yawning hole.

Brains

IT IS CHAPEL QUIET AND TWILIGHT DIM AS I ENTER CAMP Leatherneck's Concussion Restoration Care Center (CRCC), the front line of brain injury treatment. With IEDs at record levels, traumatic brain injuries are epidemic among the soldiers, along with the associated PTSD, combat stress, and emotional trauma. While armored MRAPS are reducing physical wounds from IEDs, the blast-generated pressure waves are still devastating soldiers' brains and nervous systems.

The post-9/11 wars' multiple deployments endlessly put troops in harm's way, forcing combat therapists to devise protocols for soldiers with up to thirteen brain traumas and no short-term memory. Can you imagine being on patrol with a soldier who has no short-term memory?

Until Congress pressured the generals to more aggressively treat brain injuries in late 2009, the military gave short shrift to TBIs and the associated maladies. I talked to postblast soldiers whose treatment after "getting my bell rung" was essentially aspirin and a few days' rest. Responding to the congressional pressure, the Joint Chiefs of Staff required the services to construct a standardized model of concussion care and establish frontline brain trauma clinics to speed up treatment, with the goal of getting recovered soldiers back to their units as soon as possible. In a somewhat ironic move, the military used the National Football League's evaluation and treatment protocols, though the NFL leadership also had long avoided tackling their own brain trauma scandals.

A slender naval commander emerges from the gloom. A physician from the Midwest, he's the officer in charge. Shaking my hand, he quietly tells me the clinic was established in October 2010. During the marine surge, over twenty medevacs a month were flying in TBI casualties from the Helmand battlefield. In just a few years, the CRCC treated over two thousand concussions and four thousand blast-injury cases.

Scented with disinfectant, the place is a silent, windowless sepulcher. We pad down a quilt-hung hallway as the doctor describes the TBIs caused by IEDs and other head injuries. "It creates in the brain a functional injury—a bruise on the brain," he says. "The wiring just takes a while to send its signals over—memory is slow, concentration is short." His head down, a young man very slowly, very carefully walks past us toward a ward lined with beds.

Neuropathologists report that brain trauma caused by IEDs is different from other brain injuries, such as those caused by car collisions, for instance. Victims of the IED blast injuries suffer a honeycomb pattern of broken neural connections, primarily in the frontal lobe, which controls emotions and defines personality. These IED neurotrauma victims are far more likely to experience mood swings, substance abuse, and PTSD, and they commit suicide at a much higher rate than other brain trauma patients.

The doctor says the CRCC clinicians treat the wounded soldiers with a multidisciplinary approach: primary care physicians, physical therapists, and occupational therapists collaborating on treatment, augmented by alternative medicine therapists, chaplains dispensing spiritual therapy, and combat stress teams' neuropsychologists, psychologists, and psychiatrists. "And we have a dog," the doctor smiles as a large black Labrador shambles into the room. "Hey, Joe," the doctor softly calls. "He was an EOD dog," he says about Joe's work as an explosive ordnance detection bomb dog. "Had PTSD, too, like a lot of them," Now healed, Joe wanders the clinic dispensing tail wags and compassionate understanding. "He's a great morale tool for us," the doctor says.

An occupational therapist glances up from treating a patient with a gunshot wound. "Gunshots, those are easy," the doctor says. In the far corner, a therapist talks to a soldier with an anguished look. "You might notice the light level is low," the doctor says almost in a whisper, explaining that concussion patients' heightened sensitivity to light and noise compounds their headaches and balance problems. He says the open ward also helps soldiers through the comradeship of shared recovery. "If we normalize concussions, they get better," he says.

"We've found almost everybody gets better. The computer—the brain—is very resilient, and has a miraculous way to get back its base-line." He says the CRCC clinicians monitor their patients' recovery with the Automated Neuropsychological Assessment Metrics (ANAM) test. It's a controversial screening tool. In a widely cited research report in a federal health journal, *Military Medicine*, a group of military physi-cians and researchers working in Iraq dismissed ANAM, contending that the test has "no utility" in the monitoring of long-term neurocogni-tive dysfunction.

But ANAM is the tool the military uses to get soldiers back to the battlefield. The doctor says about his patients, "We ask, 'Has the com-puter re-booted?'" Then it's a quick turn from reboot to boots on the ground: over 98 percent of the soldiers treated at the CRCC return to their units within ten days.

The doctor is enthusiastic: "It's just a fabulous facility. We're lucky to have it," he gushes. "I think overall it has served multiple purposes. Specifically, we've saved so many resources that were being expended before, sending people out of theater, losing manpower. Now we can keep it all here." Retired bomb dog Joe ambles out, sniffs, and sits down with a huff.

TWENTY

Birds

THE SOLDIERS CALL THEM BIRDS, BUT THEY AREN'T PRETTY, make-you-happy birds. Helicopters are predator birds, angry birds, devouring birds. With land travel perilous, they are often the only option. But birds exact their price.

First there's the waiting. If lucky, the two-hours-before-flight wait is in a hardened, heated PAX with racks of old, donated books. Tens of thousands of books; tons of books; reefs of books scattered across the archipelago of American bases. It's like a wildly chaotic old bookstore, run by a madman. It seems every book ever published is jumbled together: Thomas Hardy, gardening books, how-to books, Freud, Jung, a bio of Genghis Khan, pulp fiction, romantic bodice-busters, 1980s Jane Fonda fitness books, medical books, 1970s chemistry texts, cookbooks, young adult books, spiritual guides from dozens of sects and religions; many stamped with some public library's mark, from, say, a small town in West Virginia or Wyoming, a magic pass to far, far away.

More often than not, the wait is in an empty unheated tent filled with near-catatonic soldiers and contractors slumped on wooden benches. We wait in the cold; the wait of the listless, the clinically depressed. One dark, frigid morning I wait in a PAX tent crisscrossed with flexible ductwork that hangs detumescent since the sullen PAX contractors won't turn on the furnace. A frozen hour until another contractor bustles in, frowns, and switches on the heat.

There are phantom flights. Flights get overbooked. Flights get canceled. Weather. Operations. Mechanicals. You go back to your hooch. Try another day. Days go by.

Then at some point someone barks my flight number. We crouch beside the LZ (landing zone) almost in supplication, waiting for the insane beast, turning from the tempest as the bird descends. The controller waves us forward. Then there's the physical pain of humping a hundred pounds of body armor and pack across a landing zone of fist-sized rocks that threaten to twist my ankle and wreck my back as I hustle toward a great seething bird that's whining and wailing for its feeding of humans and guns. There are hot blasts from the jet engines, staggering gales of rotor wind, stinging rocks, overwhelming noise. The fear of it all overruled by the fear of not getting on. An adrenaline flare, only kept at bay with an endlessly repeated mantra: "I breathe in calm; I breathe out smile." Crew imperious, faceless in alien helmets, angrily waving us forward. Keep moving forward, spine on fire, exhausted from loads, from no sleep, from endless tension, keep moving forward, finally up the ramp, up the steps ("Engage core," I say to myself, "engage core"), and out of the vortex of pain.

Stash my gear, cram into a narrow seat, wrestle with the seatbelt (so many kinds!), get earplugs stuffed in so all hearing is not lost, and then as the bird lifts off I enter into some sort of helicopter-induced suspended animation. Meditation. Bird Land.

Sometimes cold wind rushes in from the open tail. Sometimes it's cozy with engine heat. I remember being told "helicopter" was given a Latin declension when the pope wanted to bless his new bird. Fourth declension: *helicoptorum, helicoptorum*.

A Blackhawk flight over northern Paktiya. A teeth-rattling takeoff, then an arrow-like flight over wild, dun-colored mountains, a crumpled-paper landscape of fissures and corrugations. Far down below, switchback trails lead to hidden medieval villages in ax-cleft valleys—how can we hope to conquer this? A Chinook flight over Helmand, flying through a murk of yellow sand. Blue-gray mountains gives way to barren tan ones. Scarcely anything growing. We are fighting for this?

Two British birds serenely sailing through the desert night with bellyfuls of Gurkhas, then swooping toward tiny PBS (patrol bases), one floating protectively above as the other drops soldiers and supplies. Odd, akimbo angles of the linear, cultivated landscape flowing past the open tail where the gunner is crouched beside his gun, like disorienting Fritz

Lang images in *Metropolis*. Then dreamy framed portraits of desert as the bird hovers.

On a battered marine Sea Stallion with the major, who has wisely brought big, green garbage bags. "Put your gear in the bags. Save one, cut holes for your head and arms," he counseled before we left. "Marine maintenance is shaky—birds spray hydraulic fluid everywhere." He's right. The helicopter looks old enough to have ferried marines to Khe Sanh. It's full of young marines, who don't even blink at our garbage-bag overcoats. As the bird gains altitude, hydraulic fluid sprays in a steady green mist over the marines. A doe-eyed African American marine with a sparse mustache sits at the front with his chain gun. He's impassive as a steady drip of fluid pools on his body armor. The bird sharply banks toward Lashkar Gah, the Helmand River valley asparkle with channeled water.

The marine Osprey is half copter, half plane, a bi-rotor, tilt-wing hybrid bird that has an unfortunate propensity to crash. Watching the Osprey descend to the LZ, it does indeed look like a plummeting bird of prey. I board and am barely buckled in when it flashes hummingbird-quick into the air, pausing for a second as the two C-130 motors tilt from rotors to props, shape-shifting the helicopter into a swift plane. I am suddenly looking out the open tail at the rapidly shrinking earth far below us. I remember a soldier exclaiming after a ride with hot-dogging pilots, "Sir, that was a pucker factor of nine. I thought I sucked half the seat up my asshole."

Sometimes during flights, staccato rhythms drum down the floor frame, followed by an echoing thump thump thump and the smell of cordite. Sometimes they are testing the machine guns. Sometimes it's not a test. "We own the Afghan sky," officers like to crow, but when lazy streams of tracers and hot smoke trails of rockets begin rising up from the mountains, it feels more like a very short-term lease. Silver chaff and red flares erupt from the bird, antimissile countermeasures to confuse rockets and RPGs. The taut hollow feeling, waiting for metal ripping, for screams piercing the cold air. We comfort ourselves with the thought that at least the Taliban fighters don't have Stinger missiles—yet. We fly on.

TWENTY-ONE

Geronimo

THE SURVEILLANCE DIRIGIBLE IS SAGGING OVER FOB Geronimo, a small, Hesco-warrened marine base in Helmand's Nawa-I-Barakzayi District. The large deflating aerostat seems to match the soldiers' slumping enthusiasm for the war. Both are running out of gas.

A few years before, the Taliban-governed opium-poppy stronghold of Nawa was the target of the marines' massive offensive, Operation Strike of the Sword, the corps' biggest offensive airlift since Vietnam. The surge offensive was a very expensive and bloody media event to demonstrate that the United States could shift the war's momentum. Of course it didn't. The Taliban fighters just withdrew to their Pakistan safe havens to wait out the Americans. Nonetheless, Nawa was a grand public relations victory: Chairman of the Joint Chiefs of Staff Admiral Mike Mullin strutted around Nawa without his body armor to tout the improved security. Commanding General Stanley McChrystal and President Hamid Karzai followed a few weeks later for their photo ops. It was a short photo opportunity. The Taliban were soon back, and by the next spring fighting season, McChrystal was calling Helmand "a bleeding ulcer."

The vaunted "government-in-a-box" Afghan officials are long gone, having fled for the relative security of Kabul and Lashkar Gah. Nearby Trek Nawa, the heart of darkness incarnate, is totally devoid of government presence. Now the Geronimo soldiers stand on their little bastion's defensive berms and watch the plumes of exploding IEDs all around, the dust and smoke climbing hundreds of feet into the sky. "It's so common," the major says, "you get used to them."

The major is my keeper. He's an earnest guy, exacting, hardworking, responsible. A Pennsylvania farm boy who followed the sun to South Carolina, he's got a university job when not out doing WHAM work in Helmand. He's doing his job, doing his best. The marines reluctantly approved my embed with the major's National Guard development team. But the marine PAO had a dictate: "Keep him the fuck away from my marines." So the major and I are the base's Bobbsey Twins. When I go to the DFAC, he goes, carefully steering me to tables far removed from grousing jarheads. Same for the gym, even the showers. It's tough for him—he works late into the night; I get up early. Goes that way for a few days until I suggest a deal: I will promise, absolutely promise to not talk to any marine, if he will trust me to go to breakfast, early morning work-out, and shower by myself. We are both relieved. (And I resolutely stick to my side of the bargain. I am happily the FOB Geronimo pariah, except when with my small, hospitable development team.)

The National Guard soldiers are good soldiers. Helmand may be a lost cause, but they stick to their agricultural development mission. The combat-happy marines are reluctant counterinsurgents at best. But the Pentagon ordered them to win some fucking hearts and minds, so they brought in the National Guard's citizen-soldiers to do it, damn it. The colonel who commands the team says, "When we arrived in theater, the general told us he had plenty of ideas around the AO (area of operations), but he needed some people who could execute. So that's what we're doing."

The days go by on Geronimo. The sun comes up pallid on the horizon; dust storms sweep through; stars spangle the night sky. The muezzin's call to prayer drifts over from the villages. Helicopters land; convoys head out. We line up like ants at the DFAC for our daily feedings; queue for the sputtering showers. I talk to guard soldiers trying to reconcile their long-term development mission with the realities of rapid retrograde from a failed war.

"Think of it as eating an elephant," the colonel dutifully says about his collapsing development mission. "One bite at a time." A graying West Point grad with southern-tinged accent, the colonel still parrots the jargoned platitudes of counterinsurgency-speak, the mélange of appropriated idealism and false hopes that shows up in every victory narrative

PowerPoint presentation: We are binding Afghans to their government; we're putting an Afghan face on development; we're supporting the agricultural value chain at every step; we're empowering Afghan women, improving the rule of law. And the alphabet soup of programs and contracts that will supposedly do the job: RAMP (Rebuilding Agricultural Markets Program), CHAMP (Commercial Horticulture and Agricultural Marketing Program), ASAP (Accelerating Sustainable Agriculture Program), ADP-S (Alternative Development Program/Southern Region), AVIPA (Afghanistan Vouchers for Increased Production in Agriculture), QIP (quick-impact projects), WIT (Women in Transition), on and on. It briefs well, cynical officers sneer.

The colonel is a smart man who has been in the military his entire adult life. For most of it he's been a citizen-soldier, holding down a Fortune 500 corporate job while being a Guard officer. Easy to imagine him as a solid corporate guy, rising steadily through the ranks. A product recall, some accidents, maybe a fatality or two? Stick to the talking points. A father, now a grandfather. Churchgoer. A good American. He's in the twilight of his military career, here in godforsaken Afghanistan, punching his ticket one last time. Maybe an IED will go off close enough that he can get that Combat Action Badge. Maybe if the stars align, maybe he can get that one-star rank, retire as a brigadier general. Good benefits. Stick to the talking points.

I ask, what are the challenges they encountered? His broad, lined face shadows as he haltingly talks about corruption; wasteful development projects; shrinking resources; the dangerous folly of development work in an active war zone, fighting a resilient foe supported by the populace. "I'm afraid of them," he says. "They're afraid of me."

The National Guard team's development consultant is a beefy middle-aged Midwesterner who is a veteran of all this, having begun working in Afghanistan in 2009 for USAID and beltway bandit Chemonics. "Yeah, I was part of that Mazar Food Initiative. You probably heard about that debacle," he says. It was a grandiose $30 million USAID scheme to turn a twenty-five-thousand-acre swath of northern Afghanistan into a corporate strawberry-and-goat plantation. USAID and Chemonics spent millions before finally discovering that the farm's underlying aquifer was far too saline for anything to grow. Whoopsie. The consultant laughs about the USAID officer in charge, "Yeah, he ultimately proved to be crazy." Tossed out of Afghanistan, the USAID officer continues his government career with a Latin American agricultural development project.

The consultant goes through a long list of lost causes that made a lot of people very rich. Absurdly expensive development projects run by totally clueless corporate contractors: "I met some guys, I thought 'What Mardi Gras float did you fall off of?'" Hundreds of millions dumped into battleground districts like Nawa and Marja after the surge offensive to "show some love": "How many Marja millionaires did we create?" Totally unsustainable projects; woefully implemented projects; stove-piped projects; completely insecure projects costing tens of millions, hundreds of millions. He asks incredulously, "How do you put an ag program in the south and not get killed?"

The consultant ruefully says, "Is anyone connecting the dots at this point, trying to do things differently? Not really."

: : : : :

One day I sit on the high defensive berm watching whirlwinds spin the moon dust into devils that race across the flat yellow-brown landscape. Thinking about the waste. Thinking about the sparsely resourced Taliban, still deftly checkmating the United States a dozen years after the Americans invaded with their juggernaut of military might and development money. Thinking about the Taliban's reputation for swift, fair justice in a country plagued by a systemically predatory judiciary. Thinking about the Taliban's deep connections to the egalitarian Pashtun tribal people. And sitting there above the desert, I have a Swiftian epiphany, A Modest Proposal for the Afghanistan War: Outsource the war to the Taliban. Just pay them to run it for us. The Taliban are honest and efficient, and far more effective than the kleptocratic Afghan government and the greedy US military- and development-industrial complex. Am pretty sure it will be far cheaper for the US taxpayers. And maybe the outcome will be better.

TWENTY-TWO

Dream

"LIVING THE DREAM, SIR," THE PIMPLE-FACED SOLDIER SAYS, scooting a little closer to his .50 caliber machine gun. Burrowed into a sandbagged pit at the perimeter of his besieged combat outpost, he endlessly scans the desolate terrain, his boy hands never leaving the trigger. Through the haze, Pashtun villages dot the far distance. "Reddest of the red," the officers say about the district—Taliban controlled. A Blackhawk thrums at the landing zone. Behind him, blast barriers and bullet-pocked walls. A tennis-ball-sized hole announces that the tribesmen have a recoilless rifle. The clinging stink of a burn pit drifts past. The outpost is little more than a scraped-up hillock plunked in a very bad place. Cold shower once a week, food little more than MRE (meal, ready to eat) field rations, burning their shit in fifty-five-gallon drums, relentless danger. Spec ops raid last night, two villagers killed—tribesmen say they were innocent. Reprisal's coming. "Living the dream," the young soldier repeats, glancing up with a quick smile before swiveling his eyes back. The attack came about an hour later.

Boys become warriors in that age-old way: they learn to kill; they learn to die. In their twenty-first-century wars, American soldiers learn it over multiple deployments. I sit at a DFAC table with a pale, golem-like sniper. A veteran of four rotations in Iraq and Afghanistan, he's telling wide-eyed new soldiers about zipping your buddy up in a body bag. "The eyes," he says, "looking at you as you zip it up. The eyes. That's the worst."

There is the love. They must love one another or die. They become the we, an egoless confraternity pulsing with that joyousness of puppies in a pile, their differences subsumed to their danger-annealed comradeship.

Love and fear and duty rolled into that sticky ball called courage. The shared pain. The solemn march to the airfield to see a flag-draped soldier off. How small the body when the head is gone. The quiet walk back.

War is an intense world, vivid in sensation, sharp in relief. Vital. The compression of time and distance. The honed compulsions of battle. The elation of survival. Life is better because death was near. The eternal resonance of General Lee's bittersweet remark, "It is well that war is so terrible—we would grow too fond of it."

The killing. The modern military is well equipped to train young men to dehumanize their enemies. Bad guys, the soldiers call them. The Afghans look like easy targets to soldiers habituated to killing by first-person shooter games. The enemies are abstractions. A marine medic tells me about soldiers posing with dead insurgents "like Hemingway holding up a marlin." He says, "They're just pixels on a screen to those guys."

This is nothing new. Militaries have wanted to make killing easy and abstract since the beginning, employing ever more refined training and techniques to make that happen. But killing inevitably changes humans, gives them the darkest secret, which they can only share with those among them. It's almost a trope that soldiers seldom talk about their wars with civilians. These are quiet tales told at the American Legion bar; at the brigade reunion. Certainly seldom with their families.

Deployed soldiers in the twenty-first century are always talking to their families on Skype and FaceTime—millions of love-pain packets ricocheting off the satellites. Most often it's about stuff like how the kids are doing or the broken washing machine—even if they just returned from harrowing missions outside the wire. Sometimes I can see their anguish as they stumble away from a particularly difficult call home. When I ask why they don't talk about combat, they typically say, "We don't want to worry them," or "Security."

One Memorial Day in Indianapolis I interviewed a tall, ramrod-straight marine sergeant who'd been in the bloodiest of battles in Iraq. He was there to honor one of his fallen comrades. He towered above me, the very embodiment of a warrior in his immaculate dress blues, blinding white cap and gloves, polished brass ablaze in the spring sun. He glowered, looking into the distance, disdaining to talk in more than monosyllables—until he learned I had embedded in Afghanistan. Then

I momentarily became one of the we. At least I knew something. His face softened. I asked him the question I had been asking: "Soldiers don't talk about their war experiences with their families. Why not?" He leaned down, far down, almost as if he were a tall oak bending, and then he said, slowly and intently, "Because war is just monstrous, and you don't want them to see that side of you."

Killing takes a terrible toll on soldiers across all generations and cultures. Guilt haunts them, contorts them. Traditional societies have solemn healing ceremonies to assuage soul-shadowed warriors' wrenching discordance. Today's combat veterans carry the heavy psychological burden of killing. Despite the military's perfunctory Yellow Ribbon reintegration programs, PTSD is rampant. Even as violence-glorying Americans proclaim them as heroes to be marched out at half-time shows, soldier-killers are suffering psychic wounds as old as the *Iliad* and shell shock and Vietnam Syndrome. "Moral injury" is the term their therapists use. Grave moral injury.

TWENTY-THREE

Ship

THE ROYAL MARINE BASE IS A SHIP, THE HMS *PRICE*. A BLUE painted sign by the LZ says so. By tradition, Royal Marine bases are ships, whether on sea or land. As I trudge along the HMS *Price*'s dirt roads, a ship in the desert makes as much sense as the Afghan ship of state supposedly sailing on unimpeded. Alice in Wonderland in Afghanistan. What's the nursery rhyme about a girl in a boat in a pea-green sea?

The ship, aka MOB (main operating base) Price, is a small multinational NATO base near the insurgency hotbed of Gereskh. Inside MOB Price's high, Hesco-ed walls, the Royal Marine compound includes the British Post, with an ornate cast-iron red mailbox out front. There's a small, sequestered US spec ops camp with a looming watchtower, and a district support team office where terminally degreed postnational specialists exchange homilies about Afghan development. The Danish troops have their own little battle tanks and a Scandinavian-style KFUM (Danish for YMCA) café with good coffee and two fat cats on the sun patio, where blond Danish female soldiers chat in the afternoons. There's no blare of big-screen televisions. It's as close to Euro-chic as you're going to get in Helmand.

The British tents are interconnected, hive-like structures, with netting domes and camo drapes that define each man's area. A young soldier brings in a mattress for my green canvas cot. When I thank him, he replies, "No worries." If only. The morning chatter at the latrine sinks is in American, British, and Danish, all of it mutually unintelligible.

A cosmopolitan, shaven-headed Brit, Nick, runs the DFAC, insisting his cooks prepare tasty continental fare, including English favorites such as Indian curries and steak and mushroom pie. Each night there's a table of farmstead English cheeses and, gasp, water crackers. Even the desserts are great. Given that I am now on the last notch of my belt, having lost about three inches since I landed in Kabul, desserts are on my radar. Nick sets a new standard for frontline cuisine.

But war, still. One day the major and I are negotiating the Hesco mazes when a squad of towering Royal Marine commandos in precise formation runs swiftly toward us. They are bizarre, Darth Vaderish, with black gasmasks tight on their pale, shaven heads; white T-shirts stretched across broad, muscular chests; polished black boots moving in perfect double-time unison. A phalanx of long-legged, bipedal insect warriors. "The commandos," the major says with disgust, "they are such show-offs."

In some ways, it is all for show. NATO is bolting, too. The Dutch troops left first, back in 2010. The other NATO countries were also anxious to move on. For a while, snarky comments about "European cheese-eating surrender monkeys" were briefing staples on US bases. After Obama announced the US withdrawal in 2011, it gave NATO the cover it needed. With a multinational cohesion previously not seen in the Afghanistan War, the European governments quickly followed Obama's lead, announcing rapid drawdowns of their forces.

But for the moment, the beat goes on. Though most US troops are holed up on the FOBs, there are still tentative patrols, careful to avoid casualties. There's talk that the marine commander's rules of engagement now include a focus on "less than deadly force," anathema to hard-charging jarheads. Even though there are thousands of attacks, officers are trying to sell journalists on "the improved postsurge security in the central Helmand valley," which may look true if you have blinders on and squint.

One day I'm out on a mission with the major. I'm thinking about marines patrolling during the surge with a tourniquet on each limb, ready to be tightened when they got hit. Now it's down to three tourniquets, and not even predeployed on my limbs. Before we left, the medic set me up: one's in my personal first aid kit strapped on my body armor, another's tucked under my left shoulder strap, and the cheerful red flap of a third tourniquet waves from the right pocket of my tac pants. So there, clear evidence of security progress.

But even with casualty-averse bastion tactics, there are still losses; there is still fear. One evening sober-faced soldiers begin moving toward MOB Price's front gate, where there is a vigil for a soldier who died in a suicide attack on a small patrol base. "A Brit," the major says, and turns away. "When I first arrived," he says, "I kept looking for nipples." I look at him in confusion, thinking about the Afghan women clad head to toe in enveloping burqas. "Suicide bombers," he continues. "I kept thinking if I could see the men's nipples under their shirts, they probably weren't wearing suicide vests. The suicide bombers really scare me."

It's getting to me, too. After a shower, I realize unrelenting stress and endlessly pumping adrenaline have caught up with me. I can't wash off the sharp, musky tang of fear.

TWENTY-FOUR

Slaughter

"SPEED IS OUR BEST DEFENSE," THE BRITISH SHOOTER SAYS over his shoulder as oncoming cars dodge our silver Land Cruiser hurtling down the middle of Route One. Three armored SUVs bristling with antennae and a team of malignantly cynical British security contractors heading to Gereskh at some incredible rate of speed. The driver roars to the right-hand verge and races past cars for a half mile or so, and then suddenly threads between two cars to again split the two crowded lanes. "IEDS over there," the shooter says in a thick Midland accent. Beefy, burr-headed former SAS (Special Air Service) men who'd been deployed to multiple hot spots, these shooters would be nonplussed at the gates of hell. Cars veer to the margins as we scream past. "Nice," the shooter says, and turns to grin. The driving is scary, the destination is scary, even the G4S security guys are scary.

The destination is Gereskh, the main town of Nahr-e Saraj, a Taliban stronghold for twenty years. It's the most violent district in Afghanistan's most violent province. During the last fighting season, dozens of British and Afghan soldiers lost their lives, some during bloody street battles in Gereskh, which is now in a state of sullen semiacquiescence. During the building-by-building battle, the traditional Gereskh bazaar was destroyed. The WHAM warriors then predictably let out giant contracts to rebuild it with redevelopment money. You can't parody the US war in Afghanistan. Just reporting it straight is comedy enough.

Today we are on a mission to a US-financed demonstration farm, where an Afghan government veterinarian is ostensibly demonstrating sanitary butchering techniques to tribal farmers. We are driving at very high speed to a goat slaughter.

We hit the edge of Gereskh and pass a sprawling half-constructed commercial project. Recently abandoned, it is a megalomaniac ruin of rebar-rusting ferro-cement, a twenty-first-century Xanadu. "New Bazaar," the shooter says with a laugh. I ask the development consultant about the failed project—was this USAID or British? He blinks and points to a bullet hole in the thick safety glass beside him. "Was sitting here when that happened," he says. "Pucker factor." And looks out the window. New Bazaar is clearly off the talking points.

We pass a fancy new housing estate of Afghan McMansions, typically owned by insiders with connections to the opium lords and government officials, who are often one and the same. Most often built on land stolen from the less connected. We make a quick QA/QC (quality assurance/quality controlled) stop at the construction site of the new Afghan government justice center, surely an oxymoron if there ever was one. Paid for with US tax dollars, the site is a frenzy of hundreds of Afghan workers wheel-barrowing concrete up ramps for new courtrooms, prison, and judges' apartments (because it's unsafe for them to live outside the compound). Hurry, the shooters wave us back after a cursory QA/QC moment. Can't be here too long. Insecure.

Afghan men glare at us as our convoy races down the streets. Boys throw stones with deadeye aim, clunking off the windows. "We laugh and say we ought to let them try out for the minor leagues," the major says. Just before a bridge, we careen down the bank to a dry riverbed, rooster-tailing down the wadi till the driver abruptly whips the SUV around and heads back upstream. "We take different routes to throw them off," the shooter says as he surveys the banks, pointing up at a scalable spot.

Then we begin hurtling through the center of Gereskh on lanes and alleys that are seemingly too small for these armored vehicles. I think the mirrors are going to scrape. People step back with hostile looks. Through the distortion of bulletproof glass, a ragged Afghan cityscape flashes by: turbaned men squatting in front of a tented market; bare, wintry trees silhouetted against a white adobe wall; a three-wheel motorcycle taxi with two painted hearts; enshrouded women in sky-blue and earth-brown burqas walking with perfect-postured children; open-air fabric and bric-a-brac shops pulsing with rainbow colors; vendors beside old wooden pushcarts filled with gnarled winter vegetables and mounds of bright oranges. The heavy car tilts this way and that as the driver speeds through the low, crowded town and then suddenly courses beside a shallow brown river where cloaked men walk in pairs, glancing with haughty looks as we pass. One last careen down a narrow lane, a metal gate slides open abracadabra in a high wall that we zip through, quick brake, shooters leap out with weapons ready, nod, and open the doors. We are here.

It's nice here. The Afghan government demonstration farm was formerly a royal garden. Shaded by stately cedar trees, the large walled compound is verdant with clover plots and vegetable beds flush with green cabbages, turnips, and radishes, startling after the grim, conquered city. The demonstration farm's new US-funded masonry buildings stand side by side, still smelling of fresh paint. Happy American soldiers in their body armor emerge carrying their weapons, proud of their achievement. Good, solid buildings. Check. Mission accomplished—at least until they can rotate out. Check.

An agricultural development company that feeds at the USAID money trough has the contract for the demonstration farm. "Implementing partner" is the term. It's a good gig for them, though like most of the ill-fated development projects in Helmand, it does little but feed corruption and alienate the Afghans who don't get their share. Will this absurdly expensive demonstration farm have a sustainable positive impact on Gereskh? Well, wouldn't it be lovely to think so.

Over by the new raisin-drying building, the *kishmish khana*, a group of Afghan men gather for the promised demonstration. As part of the implementing partner's contract, they are responsible for a specified number of "training" courses. It's another checkbox. In this case, an Afghan government veterinarian is going to demonstrate sanitary goat slaughter techniques to tribal farmers, whom I suspected already had a pretty good idea how to butcher goats. But surveying the crowd of natty Afghans with gold watches peeking out of their pristine *shalwar kameez*, I begin to think these guys might not actually do that much hands-on work themselves. As the government paravets tug out a large, freshly washed billy goat, the major tells me that these are twenty "power-broker farmers—influential farmers." Oh, now I get it. I ask if they get paid to attend the class. He looks at me as if I am clueless. Of course, they get paid. A very handsome payment, as it turns out. I am looking at twenty very well-connected Helmandis who are collecting their dues. A few look interested, most look bored—just here for the stipend.

It's a fast slaughter. A swift throat slice, a small geyser of rich red blood staining the turnip greens, and lop-eared Billy is soon faintly kicking meat. A paravet slits the hind leg, and blows into the skin, which balloons away from the carcass. A quick flense, brief organ talk, and the class is over. Check.

While the paravets enthusiastically hack Billy into quarters and hunks of fresh red-brown flesh, I wander off to talk to one of the British shooters keeping watch near the buildings. He's been around. What does he think of this? He glances at the spanking new farm buildings and shrugs. He asks, "But for how long?" He laughingly tells me the farm had an earlier "goat project," an expensive NATO-financed goat-breeding center—The Center for Goat Excellence or some such buffoonery. "Robustly funded," in the parlance. He tells me about the grandiose plan to import prize goats to transform the goat industry of Helmand. I ask what happened to that goat project. He smiles and says, "The goats all died." And then he laughs again.

TWENTY-FIVE

System

HAJI IS A SEASONED DEVELOPMENT CONTRACTOR, A RESPECTED graybeard Pashtun with a deeply wrinkled face. "I am old," he says in English with a sly smile. Some say eighty-four, he says sixty-eight. His age-graveled voice belies his quick mind and vibrant ways. With his turbaned crest, sharp nose, and flickering sideways glances, he brings to mind an alert raptor.

Given that he shares the same last name as a high government minister and is from the same eastern province, I am guessing Haji's also connected to a powerful Afghan official. You don't get these plum US-funded jobs unless you are. That's the way the system works. Affiliated with one of USAID's implementing partners, Haji sure knows the media routine.

He leads me on a tour of the sprawling new Nawa District Agricultural Training Center (DATC), a centerpiece of the marines' hearts-and-minds campaign after their bloody 2009 Nawa offensive. The DATC is a fairyland of American agricultural ideals and techniques; a veritable Potemkin village in Helmand. The rows of vegetables and vines are laid in military order. According to Haji, everything is "very successful." Water sparkles on the coddled plants from the elaborate drip irrigation system, which is "very successful." The large, expensive greenhouse is "very successful." The new multistory raisin-drying *kishmish khana* will be very successful—when there are actually grapes from the vines on the new American-style trellises, which, of course, will also be "very successful." (Haji clearly hasn't gotten the latest memo that trellising is out.)

Haji lauds the electric-powered pumps, the fertilizing irrigation, the intercropping, the precise plant spacing: "You see, three meters between rows, two meters between plants. And there are the keys: E and K and so on." Very organized. Very systematic. "Systematic," Haji repeats. Each row even has its own multicolor sign, listing plot and row number, plant name and variety, distance between plants, and date of planting. It's all printed in English and Pashto. All very successful—except the vast majority of Nawa farmers are illiterate. Except for that.

And except it appears that Nawa's farmers are a long way from embracing the spiffy new training facility. A long way. Spaced beside the towering, razor-topped perimeter walls, heavily armed soldiers stand watch for insurgent attack. MRAPs with machine guns in the turrets are positioned at critical corners. Two IEDs have already been planted at the DATC's newly finished gate, contradicting the promised strategic benefits of "carpet-bombing Nawa with money."

∷   ∷   ∷   ∷   ∷

"It's been a long, rough trip," the captain says about the DATC. The captain's a tall southern guy, Citadel graduate, army vet. After his service, he joined an energy company, managing nuclear projects. A family man with three young kids, he joined the National Guard after 9/11 to help out. Now he's on his third deployment and is the COR (contracting officer's representative) on the Helmand ag development project. On the record, he is upbeat about the implementing partner, and especially Haji. "He's the man who made it happen here," he says.

Off the record, he is less positive. "We're concerned about sustainability," he says. He talks about the earlier tree nursery project. "We used to give the farmers saplings. But when it turned cold, they cut the damned saplings down for wood." I wonder who in this impoverished region is going to pay for the diesel fuel to run the pumps and ventilating fans in the greenhouses when the US cornucopia is gone. Who is going to maintain these relatively complicated drip systems? It's not like the Americans can leave the instruction manuals and it will be OK. This is one of the least developed places in the world. For that matter, who's going to print up those nifty bilingual signs? When I ask the captain what he thinks will happen after the United States withdraws, he says, "I guess I am cautiously optimistic. But the hourglass is rapidly dropping and they're still insisting it is a half-full glass."

:   :   :   :   :

For sure Haji thinks the glass is half-full, pointing with enthusiasm at the fruit trees, the animal corrals, the learning center. He shows me the living quarters for the farmer-students, who need to stay overnight because of, you know, security. I ask him how well the local farmers are accepting the programming. Haji dodges, showing me a hybrid apricot tree. I try again. He points to the low greenhouses where small black cabbages are growing. "Three inches in a week!" I persist. Are local farmers accepting the government center's training and assistance? "We are training in the schools. I tell them, the gun will be finished in Afghanistan. I will be sure one by one the farmers will get training," Haji insists. One more time I ask, are Nawa farmers accepting the DATC? "No, not very good," Haji finally admits. "I don't know about the future."

But the half-full glass can yet be refilled. Haji pitches: "If the US invests more money, there will be more programs here. There will be a good result." He ticks off pomegranates, raisins, exports, touting USAID's lucrative value-chain contracts for pie-in-the-sky agricultural processing, promotion, and export programs. Of course, few of the programs ever pan out. But never mind that. For Haji's purposes, value-chain programs are the answer. This well-connected implementing partner needs a value-chain contract to keep on being very successful.

"If USA invests more money, there will be success for our country in the future," he says with a salesman's certitude. "There will be success for your county. The work is good, result is good." And Haji has one more hopeful thought: "Soon we will be working in another part of the country."

TWENTY-SIX

Believers

AFGHANISTAN HAS DOOMED THE COUNTERINSURGENCY strategy, but the believers soldier on. Some because of fixedness of mind; some because they follow orders; some because the strategy fattens their wallets—most often it's a combination of all three. Camp Leatherneck is one of the believers' last redoubts.

One night I meet with a governance and development task force that the marines organized to try to get traction in this counterinsurgency thing. It's one of those civ-mil, multiagency, hydra-headed, completely dysfunctional entities that almost define counterinsurgency in Afghanistan. Another meeting in another hardened structure; another windowless plywood room that's wall to wall with giant maps and big screens; another bunch of smart people combining to be functionally stupid.

It's another convocation of civ-mil believers spewing acronyms and buzzwords and fuzzy concepts, trying to sell plain bad ideas and hoping no one notices this has all been a total failure. These are the idea guys. It's all working out fine for them. They just keep talking. There are crisply postured military officers ballyhooing "high-quality, mission-specific" flops; dissembling diplomats and academics paying for their kids' college tuition with a year of living semidangerously; double-dipping retired military citing sketchy metrics; natty international development consultants telling marines things like "You gain more from talking to people than fighting them."

In the midst of the world's greatest opium poppy plantation, the believers say things like "We've had a reasonable amount of success in the alternative crop value chain," as though the absurdly expensive counternarcotics programs did anything but feed the government kleptomaniacs, the for-profit development corporations, and the Taliban. "There is no silver bullet here," an officer begrudgingly admits.

In a country with a wholly corrupt judiciary, the believers say, "We are focusing on a dispute resolution system. We are moving from a formal rule of law to an informal system." Which translates to mean, since the Afghan government courts are hopeless, the consultants are now recommending tribally administered sharia law courts, most likely run by the relatively honest Taliban.

And in a province that is still essentially controlled by the jihadis after a grotesquely bloody and expensive surge, the believers say, "We have improved mobility." I'm thinking about being strapped into those rolling armored bank vaults called MRAPs with machine gunners on top, and the high, nervous voices of scared young security grunts trying to negotiate the minefield of Helmand Province. Right, improved mobility.

And then, bless their pointy little heads, the believers start talking about a hearts-and-minds development offensive in the Kajaki District, which is totally Taliban controlled, so much so that the US and British military can't even deliver the concrete needed to install the multi-million-dollar hydroelectric generators that have been sitting up there for *years*. Right, send development soldiers up there to see if the Taliban farmers would like some nice wheat seed. "We are enhancing the force posture," an officer says. "Um, they have a heavy lift up there," one consultant mutters nervously. "It's a very steep hill." Another bloviates, "The model has evolved over time and the environment."

Do the believers actually believe their own delusional thinking? Probably not. Plenty of bright chatter about "moving to transition." Get out while the getting is good. When I ask about legacy, one of the advisers ventures, "Hopefully, as we withdraw, we will leave . . ." and looks away, his sentence unfinished. "Each command has different narratives," another offers.

:   :   :   :   :

I am flying out of Camp Leatherneck on the scheduled C-130 flight to Kabul. But after boarding, we wait for a long while on the runway. "A casualty," the crew tells us. Word passes down that there will be an unscheduled stop: a British soldier needs to be rushed to Bagram Air Field's sophisticated Role 3 combat hospital. So we wait through the night; soldiers sitting side by side along the aluminum fuselage, chatting about their posts, their units, their families. At long last, an ambulance pulls up at the tail ramp. We lean forward to watch, some standing to get a better view, turning to tell their comrades what they see. But as a doctor and four medics push a gurney up the ramp, the plane quiets.

The CCATT (Critical Care Air Transport Team) is moving a grievously wounded soldier. The soldier is a mummy, swathed head to toe in casts and white bandages. "Burns," the word comes down the plane, "bad burns." The soldier is comatose quiet, a sentient being whom war has transformed into an intubated organism sustained by the ventilators, flashing monitors, and snakes of saline solution and blood that surround his rolling bier. This is war, a far different war from the believers' sanitized and blithely briefed war.

The plane to Bagram is as much a cortege as a military flight. The twenty soldiers on the flight are funeral solemn, respectful of ephemeral life's sanctity. They are deep in thought.

As we fly through the cold, dark night, the hum and rumble of the plane is meditative. I begin to think about the disillusioned officers I met who can't square their loyalty to the military with the recognition that the system appropriated their honor and patriotism for a venal war. They see the worst. They know the worst.

Some are confused; some bitter; some in despair. Some have spoken out, trying to change things. Others are cynical, expressing their bottomless frustration with raspy humor. Many have resigned the service, severing themselves from who they were, knowing they will never be the same.

TWENTY-SEVEN

Rumi

SUNLIGHT STREAMS THROUGH THE GARDEN WINDOW, flooding light into the institute's cozy painted dining room. A breakfast of fresh flatbread, butter, Weetabix, and Nescafé. Next door, the Afghan cook with her elaborate Tajik headscarf is quietly humming as she sorts through small green mountains of mint and coriander piled on the kitchen floor. On the stove, pots of Afghan food are simmering, scenting the place with enticing smells.

I landed last night on the US-controlled military side of the Kabul airport. A veritable fortress with complex layers of security that eventually disgorged me into a streetscape out of a noir film. Luridly lit by the base's floodlights, abandoned buildings lined the street that stretched into the dark distance. There was no one around. The institute had promised to send a car to pick me up at the military airport's exit gate. Even had a cell conversation with the driver just before leaving the last military checkpoint. But no car. I was again not safe in Kabul.

I stood for a few minutes, trying to determine what to do. A little white Toyota taxi came toodling down the street. It was Nawab, my trusted taxi driver who drove me to Bagram when I arrived. I jumped in—so good to see him—such a relief to get off this street that was a magnet for kidnappers. Nawab whipped the car around and headed back down the street. Then he asked me where I wanted to go. And I had no idea. Didn't he know where the institute was located? Didn't they send him? He looked at me blankly. Oh, oh.

Someone else had called for a taxi, and I had taken it. Nawab spun around and sure enough there was a couple hurrying up the empty street toward us. They leapt in the taxi. They were two young American scholars working for the military, and they definitely wanted to get out of there. "Uh, this is quite the red zone," the man said, looking around. Took several more phone calls to finally figure out the problem: the institute car was waiting at another security gate, where pedestrians used to exit. Another five minutes and headlights announced their arrival. All of us were relieved.

Even though I am in a perilous city wracked by insurgent attacks and abductions, it's still great to be reprieved from US military supervision. I'm staying at an Afghan academic institute in Qale Fatullah, an ambient central Kabul neighborhood with shopping areas and two-story houses and apartment buildings. Home to a number of international NGOs, the neighborhood accordingly has popular expat restaurants and coffee shops. By developed-world standards, the city infrastructure is very basic, but after being in the primitive rural areas of the east and south, Qale Fatullah feels urbane.

I have a little private room with a wooden bed, a desk, and an Afghan rug. The bathroom's just across the hall. Given where I've been, seems quite posh. Most of the institute is unheated. Even when the temperature outside is below freezing, the front door is often open. But I have a sheet-metal *bochari* stove that's fired up twice a day when Pahlawan, the short, stocky Tajik security guard, packs it with sawdust and sets it aflame with a whoosh. Warmth, blessed warmth—for a while.

Pahlawan lives in a room beside the institute's high walls, where he fiercely guards the metal gate. With his shock of wild dark hair, soulful eyes, and line of a moustache, he looks like a weathered Omar Sharif. "He is a wrester," one of the institute's Afghan executives tells me with some pride. "He has a grandson." Pahlawan is the keeper of the place, politely knocking to tell me when a meal is ready, responding to my request for hot water for tea or my periodic sawdust blast with "Of course, of course," before hurrying off. He's married to the cook, and in the mornings before the executives arrive, they visit in the kitchen, murmurs of their interchanges drifting up the stairs. Pahlawan's deep tones are a cello line interplaying with his wife's voice, high and fluttering, like a bird moving from branch to branch.

The institute is basic, homey, and it feels like there are Afghans here who tell me the truth. Which is a nice change after traversing America's empire of lies.

:   :   :   :   :

I am dispirited and drained. I had returned to Afghanistan to find out what US counterinsurgency and development policies had changed; what were the "lessons learned." I now know the American elites didn't want to learn any real lessons, despite their failure to accomplish their stated military, diplomatic, and aid missions. The self-dealing American officials and corporate executives are acting like that is all OK. Let's take the show on the road to the next profitable hot spot. Let's keep on keeping on.

And the other disheartening problem is that I like the Afghans, a brave, creative, resilient people. What will happen to them? Sitting in my monkish little room staring at the ceiling, I ask, what does work? The money-bloated American guns-and-aid counterinsurgency sure didn't. I begin to think about finding people who have helped bring sustainable, culturally appropriate progress to poor, proud Afghanistan. What works?

Come evening I decide to walk around the neighborhood. I want to see more of Afghanistan than the view through bulletproof glass. Pahlawan opens the institute gate for me with a nervous look. I'm thinking about Afghanistan, ravaged by thirty years of war. How do the Afghans do it? How do they keep going?

It's enlivening to be out on the vibrant Kabul streets, walking with moms and dads and sisters and brothers. No body armor! I feel, well, fifty pounds lighter. The Medina Bazaar is throbbing with shoppers; chatting young Tajik women in lipstick, high heels, and headscarves; men briskly walking this way and that; housewives gathering victuals for their families. Two young boys play chess on a wooden box in front of a green-painted stall. I admire golden-brown flatbreads hanging in a brightly lit bakery window. Three bakers squat beside the underground clay oven, splatting patties of dough on the inside to bake. Someone behind me suddenly hisses, "You can't be here. You'll get kidnapped."

It's Jebrael, a young researcher from the institute. "You must go back," he says. "You can't be out here alone. Foreigners get kidnapped here." I can't bear to go back into the security bubble, so ask if he might be my guide. He gives me a big smile and says yes. So we walk the streets and lanes of Qale Fatullah. With his big, close-cropped head and quick, intelligent eyes, I can imagine Jebrael as a trusted vizier to a central Asian khan of yore; their turbaned heads together as they confer. He shows me the bazaar. We pass the Flower St. Café, an expat haven. "Many journalists go there," he says. We stick our heads in the elegant Sufi Restaurant, for patrons with solid expense accounts. We stop in at the Abdul Jamil Tamuri Fish Store, painted with pictures of giant leaping fish, seemingly odd in a dry country until Jebrael tells me they are freshwater fish from a famous Afghan lake. Just inside the open front window, the cook tends a sizzling kettle where hand-sized fish are merrily frying. The rich smell follows us onto the sidewalk. At the corner, a street vendor stands beneath a vast multicolor cloud of helium balloons. An SUV pulls up and stops, and a big red one disappears inside. We pass cordons and clots of heavily armed police and soldiers, part of the "Ring of Steel," the capital's hapless defense system. A frowning cop rushes toward me with his hand up when I stop to take a photo. Jebrael takes me past the Finest Superstore, with expensive imported foods for wealthy foreigners. Outside the entrance, impoverished women in faded burqas are begging for handouts. "They are widows," Jebrael says quietly. Beside the Superstore's security checkpoint, a guard with an automatic weapon stands ready.

Jebrael wants to show me the nearby neighborhood mosque—"very important," he says. "Very important." It's a small, modest building with a minaret that peeks above Qale Fatullah. As we pass, the muezzin's call to prayer begins to float through the cool air. Jebrael teaches me to say thank you in Dari, the Persian language of Kabul. *Tash a kor*, I repeat as we wander, *tash a kor*.

As we walk back to the institute, a sickle of a moon is rising. We stop to admire it framed in the dark silhouette of cloud-like conifers. Looking up at the numinous orb, Jebrael points and says, *"Ma,"* Dari for moon. On a dangerous street in this war-ravaged city, he recites Rumi's thirteenth-century poetry: "At night, I open the window and ask the moon to come and press its face against mine." I am suddenly looking at the moon differently, a scimitar of light hanging above a pine tree's dark serrations. The world shifts from menacing to enchanting.

We walk on, negotiating the piles of black ice and packed snow, dodging the anarchic traffic, avoiding the large rectangular holes that punctuate the heaved and cracked sidewalks, all the while talking about Afghan poetry. Jebrael tells me about Rumi's enduring appeal to contemporary Afghans (as I indeed confirm when other Afghans spontaneously quote Rumi to me). He tells me about the "local and beautiful" informal Dari poetry, and I tell him about the expressive Pashtun and Taliban poetry that others shared with me. I recite a line I remember: "The sight of God rests on high mountains." Sauntering along under the moon, I consider the solace and splendor that poetry bestows on Afghans, and how ancient cadenced words inspire their enduring courage and spirit.

TWENTY-EIGHT

Enduring

SNOW-DUSTED KABUL IS TRANSFORMED INTO A COLD, WHITE confection. When I arrive at Bagh-e Babur, the world-renowned Babur's Gardens, a lone workman is sweeping the thin white layer off the stone courtyard in front of the caravanserai's long, arched colonnades. Skeletal trees stand sentinel. The great Muslim conqueror, Babur, ordered the gardens built as a pleasure retreat soon after conquering Kabul in the early sixteenth century. More than five hundred years later, Babur's magnificent formal gardens rise above me. The place is deserted.

I walk up a long flagstone avenue through a terraced masterpiece, past water flowing down a grand channel of white marble. As I admire the gardens, a sturdy gray-haired man in a sagging gray sport coat, gray striped sweater, a layering of shirts, and pale-gray wide-wale corduroy pants ambles down the stairs. We exchange hellos. When I say, "What a beautiful garden," he lights up and replies, "When someone says this is a beautiful garden, Persians say, 'You have beautiful eyes.'"

The garden's director is surveying his fiefdom. During the summer the gardens are thronged with Kabulis, up to sixty thousand on a busy day. But today I am it, and he is eager to show a visitor his beloved Bagh-e Babur. He tells me the grounds were laid out in the classical Persian *chahar bagh* (four garden) pattern, the quartered garden terraces bisected by the main watercourse, which carries water down from the mountains to feed burbling channels, basins, fountains, and cascades that interplay with pavilions and tombs of exalted people. He points out the spreading plane trees, the green conifers, and pomegranates bundled up for the winter. He says they also have walnut, cherry, quince, mulberry, and apricot trees, which were also planted in Babur's original garden. Given Islam's origins in the hot, arid desert, it's not surprising that traditional Islamic gardens always feature water and shade for rest and relaxation. The director tells me the Koran teaches that gardens are an earthly reminder of paradise. For Babur, this was heaven on earth.

Descended from both Timur and Genghis Khan, Babur was destined to conquer. Born in the Fergana valley in what is now Uzbekistan, Babur started cutting a wide swath at a young age. Taking the crown of Fergana at eleven, he conquered Samarkand at fifteen. He had his ups and down, but through his campaigns in the Indian subcontinent, he laid the foundations for the Mughal dynasty. Babur was India's first Mughal emperor. When Babur died at the age of forty-seven after a lifetime of world-changing conquests, his gardens became his final resting place.

The director tells me he was an Afghan army colonel during the Soviet and the Najibullah communist government war against the US-supported mujahideen. "We made one mistake," he says, "we turned our weapons over to the mujahideen. But it was a decision made by the generals, not the people, not the soldiers. We gave them our tanks, our air force. The army is strong now. They won't do that again."

He looks at me and says, "I believe in our government, but not our leaders. They are mafia, all mafia. And I am sorry, sorry, but your government did that. Mafia."

Like many Afghans I speak with, the director laments that Afghanistan lost its golden opportunity when the international community rushed in with open wallets. "All wasted," he says. "The money's all gone to the mafia, the Karzai mafia."

He tells me he is fifty-four. I tell him I have two sons in their forties. He looks surprised. "How old are you?" Sixty-three. We laughingly agree we both are quite vital and look great for our ages. Big, open smile, his eyes crinkling behind his horn-rims. He says, "Afghans know Americans and Europeans only have one or two sons, but they still send them to help us. Afghans know Americans and Europeans are paying taxes and sending money to help us. We know this. But little money has gotten to the Afghan people."

The director shows me the elegant white marble mosque that Babur's descendant, Shah Jahan, built after he completed the Taj Mahal. We

climb toward the top of the garden, which has a wide vista of Kabul and
the surrounding snowcapped mountains. It's been an auspicious spot for
a long time. Archeologists discovered that the site had monumental
buildings dating back to the third century BC, and Timurid tombs that
predated Babur's by many centuries. In the centuries following Babur's
interment, the Indian Mughal emperors used the gardens to express
their political power and connection to their mountain homeland.

The gardens continued to resonate political importance. In the late
nineteenth century Amir Abdur Rahman, the "Iron Amir," as the British
called him, instituted a massive building project here, adding additional
pavilions and watercourses, as well as a sprawling haramseray. King
Nadir Shah reconfigured major parts of the gardens in the 1930s to provide an airy European-style park for the Kabuli general public.

During the wrenching Afghan civil war in the 1990s, rockets and
shells rained down on Kabul, destroying 80 percent of the city and killing as many as fifty thousand civilians. The gardens on high ground had
strategic importance. "This was the front lines," he says, and tells me of
the battles between the tribal warlords, Massoud, Hekmatyar, Dostum,
and Sayyaf among them. After the Taliban triumphed in the mid-1990s,
the gardens were essentially wrecked. The few remaining buildings were
pocked with bullet holes. Countless fruit trees, including many mature
almond trees, were cut for firewood. The plantings had long since withered and died. He shows me the stump of a massive plane tree that died
when irrigation was cut off.

After the post-9/11 US invasion, an international cultural consor-
tium began work on Babur's Gardens. Spearheaded by Aga Khan Trust
for Culture, reconstruction started in 2003. Afghans labored one hundred thousand workdays to rebuild the gardens' high, defining walls and
its approximately twenty-seven acres of formal gardens. Babur's tomb
was restored to its imperial glory. "Would you like to see?" the director
asks. We climb to the top terrace to Babur's final resting place, high over
Kabul.

As befits a nomad king, Babur wanted to be buried under the open
sky. So his grave is uncovered, a small, refined marble tomb standing
amid a surround of graceful pierced marble screens that his descendant
Shah Jahan erected. The garden director points to the Mughal emperor's

inscription: "Only this mosque of beauty, this temple of nobility, constructed for the prayer of saints and the epiphany of cherubs, was fit to stand in so venerable a sanctuary as this highway of archangels, this theatre of heaven, the light garden of the god-forgiven angel king whose rest is in the garden of heaven, Zahiruddin Muhammad Babur the Conqueror."

"Babur's family still comes," the director tells me. "Not too many years ago, some of his family came from the Fergana valley. They are Uzbeks. They wanted to roast a lamb. They had a party here." I am intrigued. What was the legacy of this great conqueror, this founder of the Mughal Empire? How does power flow down through the centuries? I ask what kind of people they were. Were Babur's descendants still powerful? He smiles and shakes his head. "No, no," he says. "They were very simple people. Very simple."

TWENTY-NINE

Beauty

THE BOMBED-OUT PALACE LOOMS OUT OF THE SLEET, STANDING wraithlike high above the National Museum of Afghanistan. Decades after its destruction during Afghanistan's internecine wars, the European-style Darul Aman Palace is still in ruins. Built in the early 1920s as part of King Amanullah Khan's doomed modernization efforts, the imposing palace known as Afghanistan's Versailles stood empty for decades after the Islamic conservatives forced the king from power. Restored in the 1970s and 1980s by the modernizing Soviet-backed government, the building again became the target for fundamentalists, this time by mujahideen factions vying for control of Kabul during the civil war. Just a year before my little white taxi skittered below, the Taliban attacked the ghostly, gutted neoclassical structure. Some symbols just never stop being good targets.

It takes three trips to the far western outskirts of Kabul to finally find the National Museum open. Once one of the world's great museums, it housed over one hundred thousand objects from Afghanistan's history at the crossroads of the ancient world. But the museum also suffered the depredations of wars. During the civil war, fighters looted the collection several times before destroying the building with rocket fire in 1994. By then only about 30 percent of the collection remained. Most of the loot was sold into the illicit international art market, including the legendary Bagram Ivories, the Kunduz Hoard of Greco-Bactrian coins, and ethereal Gandharan Buddhas. In the midst of the chaos, the devoted museum staff removed the most important remaining objects, including the invaluable Bactrian gold, to secure locations in Kabul. When the Taliban took power in the late 1990s, they had a short-lived tolerance for Afghan cultural heritage, including pre-Islamic cultures. In August 2000, the Taliban reopened the museum. But historic Afghan culture soon became a pawn in global geopolitics as the US-led embargo of Afghanistan led Taliban senior officials to abruptly change their policy. The infamous destruction of the towering Bamian Buddhas followed. Fundamentalist zealots connected to the ill-named Ministry of Culture also rampaged through the closed museum, destroying pre-Islamic Afghan art that they considered to be graven.

As I walk into the two-story brick building, I feel like I am visiting a battleground. I am seeing beauty and history under siege; beauty and history passionately defended. That it is here at all is a testimony to human dedication. Near the security checkpoint, I notice a plaque that reads, "A nation stays alive when its culture stays alive."

While much of the looted art has not been found, the museum still has a treasure trove of objects from Afghanistan's rich and varied past: Stone Age and Bronze Age artifacts, finely carved third- and fourth-century Greco-Bactrian Buddha heads, an elegant Gandharan stucco Buddha with a beatific gaze, ancient Roman glassware and Chinese mirrors, a fifteenth-century black marble Kandahari basin carved with lotus leaves, and elaborately carved Kabuli doors. I'm fascinated by the eerie life-sized carved wooden grave monuments from the animistic Nuristani region of remote northeastern Afghanistan, a relic of the *kafir* (unbeliever) culture that flourished in the high, steep mountains long into the nineteenth century.

I stop to admire one of the museum's treasures. The Rabatak Tablet was found in 1994 by a mujahideen digging a defensive trench near the Kabul–Mazar highway. Written in Bactrian script, the tablet sings the praises of Kanishka, "the righteous, the just, the autocrat, the god," one of the Kushan kings who ruled the thousand cities of Bactria. Once the tablet was found in the late twentieth century, it continued to be a signifier of power. A British demining technician working in the area sent a photograph of the tablet to the British Museum, where experts determined its Kushan origin and translated the inscription. Because of the anarchy, British experts weren't able to travel to Afghanistan to see the irreplaceable object until 2000, when they found it stacked in a Department of

Mines and Industry warehouse in the north. A few months later, officials transported the half-ton stone tablet to Kabul, where it was the centerpiece of the Taliban's museum reopening. After Taliban hardliners closed the museum, the Rabatak Tablet went into storage, and the widespread destruction of the unbelievers' art began.

All of the lost history and destruction begins to cast a pall as I walk through the sparse galleries. My solitary footfalls; the threadbare building; the dispirited staff; the patched-together statues, some quite literally defaced, all add to my mood.

There are exhibits celebrating Afghanistan's vibrant thousand-year Buddhist heritage, as well as its Greek and Islamic cultures. I learn about the artistically rich eleventh-century Islamic Ghazni Empire that ruled the vast regions between Kabul and Kandahar from its strategic position between the Persian world and India's Indus valley. Inspired by the subtle poetry and art of the Persian courts, Ghaznavi rulers encouraged a literary and artistic flowering that influenced culture as far away as India. Honoring its three thousand years of culture, IESCO, the Islamic Educational, Scientific, and Cultural Organization named Ghazni the capital of Islamic civilization for 2013. Given the violent insurgency in Ghazni, I question how many cultural tourists will make the trip.

Another gallery displays artifacts from the Mes Aynak site south of Kabul. Located along the ancient Silk Roads, Mes Aynak is one of Afghanistan's most important sites, continuously inhabited since the Bronze Age. It was a thriving city through the Buddhist second-century Kushan period and well into the early Islamic period after the religion reached Afghanistan in the eighth century. The artifacts that the archeologists found are stunning, confirmation of Afghans' amazing artistry. But Mes Aynak is another casualty of geopolitics. In their omnivorous search for raw materials, the Chinese have obtained the rights (reportedly with massive bribes) to a gargantuan mining concession at Mes Aynak, which will ravage the site. The extraordinary artifacts I am viewing are coming from a hurried, last-ditch archeological salvage operation.

Afghanistan, it is all for sale. And the museum seems to be illustrating that all is finite; all is impermanent. Grand empires that lasted centuries: Greco-Bactrians, Mauryans, Kushans, Saffarids, Samanids, Ghaznavids, Ghurids, Timurids, Mughals, Hotakis, Durranis—reduced to dusty artifacts on museum shelves. I leave wondering what American detritus will be on the museum shelves in centuries to come—piddle packs and rusted MRAP parts?

:   :   :   :   :

The Kuchi carpet store is in the ancient caravanserai. It's like walking into Ali Baba's cave, finely woven carpets in jeweled colors covering the old herringboned brick walls up to where they curve into great flat arches. Antique brass oil lamps. Rustic chip-carved doors. Abdull emerges from behind one of the mounds of folded carpets, hand on heart, saying *salaam alaykum* (peace be unto you). *Salaam*, I reply and soon am perched on a small wooden stool drinking green tea as Abdull tells me about his carpet-dealer uncle who started the company, taking the highest-quality Afghan carpets to Europe. A slender, bareheaded young man with a fringe of a beard, Abdull mingles Afghan and European with his green tweed sport coat and wool V-neck sweater over a traditional white *shalwar kameez*. He shows me one of his uncle's museum-quality Afghan rugs in the glossy British textile-collectors' magazine, *Hali*. "Auction," Abdull says, "Geneva."

They feature the carpets of the Kuchi, the nomads who traverse great swatches of Afghanistan and surrounding countries herding their flocks of sheep, goats, and camels, and weaving their traditional tribal rugs on their portable looms. Rugs of Afghanistan begin unfurling before me: Dazzling Baluchs, intricate Turkomans, rare rugs from the northwest, prayer rugs, tasseled saddlebags, runners, enormous room-sized carpets, flat-weave kilims, new rugs from Herat, old, old, fragile carpets— "not for sale," Abdull says before carefully refolding, "for museum." Hand-woven medallions, curlicues, paisley-like *botehs*, and angular flowers called *guls* intertwine with meandering vines, stylized leaves and trees, all bordered with the geometrics of the ancient Persian world. The intense beauty of natural dyes—the red of madder and cochineal shells, blue of indigo, orange of henna, oak-bark brown, hollyhock purple. War rugs for the tourists: woven attack helicopters, tanks, grenades and AK-47s; one with the Twin Towers burning and flaming missiles aimed for the map of Afghanistan.

Some cups of tea and many rugs into the afternoon, Abdull and I parlay over a vivid Baluch carpet of purple, blue, and red, and a small, old, brown Kuchi rug that's crude and rough and feels like it was woven in a hundred camps across the wild plains and deserts of western Afghanistan.

:   :   :   :   :

"I will wait," my taxi driver says as I get out next to the river in the Murad Khane District, a Shia area in the heart of old Kabul where a few years before a suicide bomber killed seventy people at the Abu Fazl Mosque during the Ashura commemoration. "Over there," he says, nodding to the river side of the street. "You call before you come out," holding up his cell phone. White smoke billows from a narrow brazier filled with skewers of lamb. The Hazara with the red apron tending the fire in front of his jade-green storefront stares at me as I walk toward the high wooden gates of the Turquoise Mountain Institute for Afghan Arts and Architecture.

Started in 2006 with the support of Prince Charles and diplomat-adventurer Rory Stewart, the institute was established to regenerate the ramshackle historic neighborhood and provide a locus for Afghan traditional arts. Murad Khane's origins date back to the eighteenth century, when a nervous Afghan king enlisted Turkic Shia mercenaries, the Qizilbash (Red Hats), to strengthen his forces. This was their citadel. In the ensuing centuries, as the mercenaries' descendants became administrators, clerks, traders, and artisans, the area was a center of learning. Time was not kind to Shias in Sunni-dominated Afghanistan, and prejudice and oppression were common. When the work began in 2006, the ancient walled redoubt was impoverished, without running water, sewers, or electricity. The wooden houses were in ruins, nearly buried under six feet of garbage.

The project enlisted the community to clean, restore, and improve the area. "We employed every single person in this area," the Brit says. "It was blanket employment." A trim, well-dressed development consultant with stylish horn-rimmed glasses, he's focused on using the arts to regenerate societies. He's one of only two foreigners among the

350 Afghans working at Turquoise Mountain. After the local workers removed thirty thousand truckloads of rubbish, well over a hundred structures were restored. Antique wooden buildings with their fine *pa-tayi* arcade screens, *panjare* latticework windows, and balconies and doors intricately carved with arabesques again became the domiciles of learning and culture. The neighborhood now has electricity and water, a school providing education to boys and girls, and a new health clinic that treats thousands yearly.

The institute established a school of Afghan arts, including wood-working, calligraphy, jewelry, ceramics, and textiles. Beyond artisanal skills, the students are taught design and business. Some of Kabul's best artisans became the teachers. The institute found one of the last masters of ornate Afghan chip carving and joinery selling bananas in the market. He'd achieved renown for the elaborate ceilings and windows he carved for the presidential palace. Now a stooped and bright-eyed eighty-five years old, he passes on his knowledge to students in the sun-shafted workrooms. As a saw rasps, the air is perfumed with the scent of cedar.

There's a steady sound of dripping eaves as we cross a snow-dusted flagstone courtyard, the bright sun winkling the icicles. We climb sets of steep, narrow steps past wooden window screens pierced with painstaking *jali*-style carving. In the calligraphy studio, a trio of young Afghan women sits on the wooden floor artfully swashing arabesques on the thick sheets of creamy handmade paper, painting phrases of the Qur'an and epic poems of conquest and love. One reads, "Love turns thorns into roses." A student looks up from her painting, her brush hovering above a paint pot of azure. "Because of my special interest in calligraphy and painting, I joined Turquoise Mountain," she says. "I am hoping my interest will be to give me a good future."

There's a whine of a foot-powered grinder in the jewelry atelier, the rasp of a fine file, tap of a hammer. We pause before a slowly whirring grinder, where a student is polishing a gem as he pedals. "Traditional Afghan," the Afghan guide says. "Very good. No need for electricity." "We try to focus on what they have," the Brit says. "And what the Afghans do have is loads of gems." Around me I see the cool blue of lapis lazuli, Arabic for "stones of the sky." The Afghans have been mining lapis for over six thousand years, since the Sumerian kings discovered thick veins high in the northern Hindu Kush, mines that are still in operation. Emeralds, rubies, and sapphires twinkle in the glass cases. Jewelry set with Afghan amethyst, peridot, garnet, tourmaline, aquamarine, and topaz is nearby. As traders since the days of Ur have known, Afghanistan has gems.

The head of the jewelry workshop is from a family of jewelers. His father was the king's jeweler. "The shah, he worked for the shah, and he taught the students," the head jeweler says. "This is my own," he says handing me an elegant ring set with a large lapis flecked with tiny glints of white. "That is natural," he says.

"My job is to put the artisans in touch with international designers," the head of international development tells me. An Afghan expatriate who was educated in Britain in art, design, and architecture, the woman came to Kabul to help with Turquoise Mountain after hearing Rory Stewart speak in London. "Kate Spade came to Kabul in 2009, and was quite keen to work with Afghan jewelers." Spade designed a line of jewelry highlighting the stones of Afghanistan, and ordered a large lot for her upscale Manhattan store. "They have been quite popular. We recently delivered her re-order. It was $22,000." Turquoise Mountain also sells the pieces in their gift shop. "The prices we charge here are very different from what they charge in New York," she giggles. "But it's Kabul, so we can do that. We try not to undercut Kate Spade, but not too many people get to Afghanistan."

She tells me that Turquoise Mountain is changing its focus, moving from direct production and sales to helping their graduate Afghan artisans forge independent relationships with the international designers and clients. "They can price them the Afghan way, because they don't have to deal with a big overhead. It makes their prices a lot more competitive," she says with a smile. "What makes me so happy about this is that it makes the system a lot more sustainable. Because at some point, we are all going to leave."

THIRTY

Sustaining

THE GRANDMOTHER OF AFGHANISTAN IS EXASPERATED. Legendary archeologist, ethnologist, and activist Nancy Hatch Dupree has spent a half a century earning her moniker, working with the king, the communists, the warlords, the Taliban, and now the Americans and their NATO allies. And she is appalled at what's happening to her adopted country. Long a critic of the "so-called experts and advisers" who thundered into Afghanistan to take advantage of the avalanche of postinvasion development money, Dupree condemns their pernicious impact. She says, "I'm seeing in the last years too much money, too many outsiders making decisions, and they are undermining one of the best characteristics of the Afghans, which is self-sufficiency; the pride in being able to be self-sufficient. They've undermined that."

We're at Dupree's Afghanistan Center at Kabul University (ACKU), which is dedicated to researching and preserving Afghanistan's rich cultural heritage. The center's new building is part of the Louis and Nancy Hatch Dupree Foundation, which carries on the work of Louis Dupree, the preeminent ethnographer and archaeologist of Afghanistan. Author of the magisterial compendium *Afghanistan*, Dupree celebrated the wisdom and culture of the Afghans, from their prehistoric past to their thriving tribal present.

Knowing the independent and contentious Afghans as he did, Louis Dupree long advocated for a decentralized federal system of government for Afghanistan. He knew a unitary government centered in Kabul would have little chance of surviving the country's unending tribal unrest. In his view, a layer of semiautonomous regional entities would absorb much of the internecine conflict, letting a relatively weak central government act as a mediator between the perennially squabbling tribesmen. The Kabul-centric unitary government that the US-led coalition imposed on the Afghans with the postinvasion constitution sure hasn't worked. All it did was centralize the graft. Louis Dupree is probably laughing somewhere.

With her small frame, high cheekbones, and nimbus of white hair, Nancy Hatch Dupree is reminiscent of a wizened leprechaun, albeit a curmudgeonly, salty-tongued one. Born in 1927, she talks a high-pitched, quavery voice tinged with a slight southern-ish accent, speaking in verbal bolds, italics, and exclamation points. She's outspoken, articulate, and mad as hell about the wasteful international development efforts that destabilize Afghanistan, her opprobrium delivered in a voice quivering with indignation. She asks, "Why don't they think of basics? They think too big. Big dams, agriculture, drug programs. Too much money." She gives failing scores to the US development programs: "I give them two, on a scale of ten. These huge projects, you do not make improvements overnight. It takes a long time to change peoples' thinking. These traditions that are in use, why should we impinge on them? You will not change them overnight just by screaming or throwing money. You sit down with them over a cup of tea, and work with them."

And just as passionately, she expresses her deep respect for the Afghans' ability to handle things in their own way, not at the whim of some self-dealing international development consultant. Following her faith, Dupree organized the Libraries in a Box program, which ships small lending libraries of books to remote, rural areas, where illiteracy levels are high, but the people are hungry for knowledge. The books are packed in sturdy wooden boxes for transport to these rugged regions—in some cases on the backs of donkeys. "It's a sustainability project," she says. "I noticed that the international donors funded all these adult literacy programs—without one cent for books. Without books, the adults quickly lose their new reading skills."

Dupree relies on the Afghans to tell the ACKU what books they want. "People in the rural areas aren't *stupid*," she exclaims. The readers often request practical books, such as on health, management, animal husbandry, and farming. But there is also a great demand for books on Afghan history. Lately, the readers want books on computers and technology.

Responding to readers' requests, the ACKU staff produces and publishes small volumes on diverse subjects. "They wanted a book, why does Afghanistan have so many earthquakes? So we did one," Dupree says.

"I was told this was the *stupidest* project that was ever thought, because I wouldn't have a book left in six weeks. Everything would be stolen. Now it just makes me *laugh*." She tells me the lending libraries have miniscule losses. "The few that are lost are mainly due to *too much use*," Dupree says with an impish smile.

When she first came to Afghanistan in the early 1960s, she was a young American foreign service wife. Bored with embassy social life and intrigued by the country, she set out to write Afghanistan's first guidebook. Seeking the advice of an American archeologist, she dropped off her manuscript with Louis Dupree. "Well," she says, "Louis indicated my book was 'adequate, but nothing original.' I turned to leave, but he said 'come back here,' and so I went back—and never left. Oh, it was a *scandal*."

The Duprees became swinging Kabul's glamorous power couple during the city's liberal heyday in the 1960s, Nancy writing guidebooks and Louis digging, researching, and writing. "It was a charming little city," she says, "with a lot of elegant entertaining." Their "five o'clock follies" cocktail parties were part of the Kabul high life.

After the Soviet-supported leftist government took power in 1978, the Duprees were deported. The Duprees settled in Peshawar, the Pakistani border town near the Khyber Pass that seethed with jihadist intrigue, where Louis Dupree assisted the US government's support of the Islamic fundamentalist mujahideen during the 1980s Soviet war. While in Peshawar, they began to gather the documents relating to Afghanistan that were in danger of being lost, including NGO reports, mujahideen newspapers, and records relating to the US intervention. Louis Dupree died in 1989, but Nancy continued their curatorial work in Peshawar.

The US invasion of Afghanistan after 9/11 changed her situation. She could think about returning to Kabul. She had another literary moment in 2002 when playwright Tony Kushner used her *Historical Guide to Kabul* as the inspiration for his play *Homebody/Kabul*. While the United States and its allies were ostensibly in control in Afghanistan, it wasn't until 2005 that she thought it safe to bring the invaluable Dupree collection back, smuggling it into the country in three hundred old seed bags. "Not one single sheet was lost," she says, her voice rising in triumph.

When she returned to Kabul, guns-and-aid money was inflating the city into the Kabubble. She saw the international developers building hundreds of schools and clinics with little local buy-in and no money for programming, so the projects often failed. "Clinics without equipment," she sneers. "Schools without teachers." So she determined to build a home for the Afghan collection with ongoing programming, organized to serve as an intellectual center for rising Afghan scholars to sustain Afghanistan's culture. She reached out to a broad range of people and organizations. She persuaded Kabul University to donate the land, and cajoled the Afghan Finance Ministry into paying for the construction.

Inspired by traditional Afghan architecture, the new ACKU center has thick, rough-hewn stone walls, reflecting the high defensive walls of fortlike *qalats*, the typical farm compounds in the rural areas. The building's white marble was quarried near Kabul. The gargantuan wooden support beams are from the Taliban stronghold of Kunar Province. Dupree tells me that her friend Hamid Karzai got the giant cedar logs released after they were confiscated from illegal loggers. "Not one tree was logged for this building," she brags.

The interior of the building is clearly a twenty-first-century space, with research facilities and high-end networked computers. The Dupree collection, now augmented by thousands of other Afghan-related documents and books, is housed in climate-controlled libraries, where librarians are preserving the material for future generations. "Cataloging and digitizing," she calls to the scholars, who smile in return at their grandmother.

Like a *qalat*, where much of the Afghan life goes on inside the protective walls, the ACKU offices, labs, and libraries surround an internal courtyard. As we move through the building with its large interior windows, Dupree stops again and again to look into the sunny courtyard, where a group of young men and women are gathered for a meeting. They are among the ninety-three Afghans on the ACKU staff—"my family," she calls them. She tells me that the ACKU is focused on building research skills in a country where those have been in short supply. And Nancy Hatch Dupree sees the ACKU's traditional Afghan courtyard as a place where the scholars can share their new skills and plot their own future. She says with a soft smile, "These young Afghan people, they need to determine their own pathways."

THIRTY-ONE

Challenges

EVERYTHING SEEMS CHALLENGING. IS THIS FOOD SAFE; THAT bridge mined? Is that a secure location to meet? Is that person trustworthy? Is that boy hurrying toward me with a pressure cooker in his wheelbarrow a suicide bomber or just a curious kid? There's the spiraling nebula of embed approvals; public affairs officers sticking to the talking points; the State Department handling interviews requests like IEDs—potentially explosive events requiring much time-consuming consideration. Take a number. Get back with us.

But for some reason, the Afghanistan foreigner registration card causes me the most anxiety. Getting the card when I arrived at the Kabul International Airport from Dubai should have been simple: guidebooks counsel bringing two passport photos and a passport copy to the office just behind the baggage claim, where an official will issue the registration card. Simple. But like most things in Afghanistan, simple is never simple, because the office wasn't open when my flight arrived in Kabul. I knew I needed that rubber-stamped registration card to fly out of Afghanistan, but intent on getting to my embeds, I decided to worry about it later.

Later is now. The lack of a foreigner registration card is looming large in my fervid imagination—I am conjuring rapacious Afghan officials detaining me as my flight is boarding. I want to go home. I need the card. Then I learn the *other* way to get the registration card is to go to the Ministry of Interior Affairs' registration office in downtown Kabul—a "major hassle," the guidebooks promise.

A kind Afghan assures me it is no problem. He will go with me. So one morning we're off to the Ministry of Interior Affairs. It's the standard

departure from the walled and razor-wired guesthouse: We climb into
the SUV and wait. Pahlawan peers out the high metal gate's peephole. "A
wrester," the Afghan tells me again. Nodding to us, Pahlawan activates
the gate, and we sweep into the narrow street before it is completely
open. I can see it closing before we are out of sight.

It's another helter-skelter ride through anarchic traffic, the Afghans'
ubiquitous little Toyota sedans mixed up with the powerfuls' gun trucks
and armored SUVs. My driver is deftly dodging cars speeding from every
direction: city-scale vehicular chicken. Cat Stevens's hit "Wild World"
starts playing in my head. Cars with large decals on the rear windows:
"Power is nothing without control. Trust no one." A common one in
this gender-segregated town: "No Girls No Tension." Rolling down one
residential street, two SUVs suddenly veer across both lanes to block the
street. Tall, sun-glassed shooters leap out with automatic weapons, scanning the traffic and surrounding buildings. A gate slides open in a high
masonry wall, a polished black SUV heavy with armor lumbers into the
compound, the shooters give one last warning glance before following.
At the next intersection, the traffic flows around another clutch of heavily
armed shooters intently surveying the rooftops. Diplomats and legal
experts talk about Afghanistan's failed rule of law. Trust me, you can see
it on Kabul's streets and highways. If I get PTSD, it's traffic related.

⋮ ⋮ ⋮ ⋮ ⋮

Looming over a traffic-clogged avenue, the Ministry of Interior Affairs'
headquarters is a decaying ferro-cement complex with all the charm
of an ancient prison. Crowds of Afghans throng the security gate as
cars and carts disgorge more. Inside the courtyard, a surging mob pulses
amoeba-like around an entrance. (Afghans have not embraced queuing
as best I can see.) My guide says the Afghans are here to get their *tazkiras*,
the recently mandated biometric identity cards.

My guide directs the driver to drop us off near a security checkpoint,
telling him to stay close. He will call. Dipping his shoulder to enter the
crowd, he negotiates the checkpoint and makes a beeline to an office off
to one side, glancing back to be sure I'm in his wake. I jostle and thread
my way behind him. A very small, faded sign on the door reads, "Foreign

Registration." I can only imagine how long it would have taken me to find the office. Just inside the door, a wizened dwarf sits imperiously behind a desk sorting piles of foreigner registration cards. Half-hidden by a large black turban and a red-and-black neck scarf that almost reaches his mouth, his wrinkled face is a mask of disapproval. He purses his lips. He glares. His tiny feet swing below his chair in barely bottled frustration. He barks Dari in a high, singsong voice at the three young functionaries crowded into the unlighted cell with him.

One points us toward a divan at the end of the room, where an older Afghan in a wool Panjshiri hat waits in the gloom. I fill out the application and hand the boss my paperwork. He translates my form into Dari, and fills out a registration card. While he carefully trims one of my photos with a pair of battered red shears, I notice a typewritten sign on the wall, addressed to "My dear esteemed foreign visitors and their colleagues," notifying all that the foreigner registration card is "free and gratis" and no one should ask for payment. No one does.

Then it's back through the courtyard throng to a building on the other side. The hall is Afghanistan in review: elegant Tajik women in head scarves and narrow high-heeled platform shoes, Haraza men looking like the Great Khan's men, a team of stolid Uzbeks, Westernized young swains in suit coats, Pashtuns with cockscomb turbans, diminutive women hidden beneath blue thousand-pleat burqas, an understory of self-assured, clear-eyed children.

My guide sweeps into an upstairs office, where he directs me to give the bureaucrat my passport and card. I no more than hand them to him before he pushes past me into the melee. As I lose sight of him and my passport, I think, "Oh, darn—so close," and begin mentally preparing myself for replacing my stolen document. But suddenly he's back, waving me into another office, this one with the magical sign: "Foreign Registration." A second later, an official behind a desk takes a moment from his conversation to reach into a drawer for his stamp. Bam! It's done.

"Let's go," my guide says.

THIRTY-TWO

Women

THE AFGHAN WOMEN ARE EAGER TO TELL THEIR STORIES.
Entrepreneurs all, they are gathered around the table at Kabul's American University, leaning in as they wait their turn. All proper Muslim women, their heads are politely scarfed. They are nicely dressed. Most are educated, from progressive families. They are part of a Goldman Sachs–sponsored development program, "10,000 Women," established in conjunction with the Thunderbird School of Global Management to increase the numbers of successful women entrepreneurs in dozens of developing countries around the world. The State Department and USAID support the project.

The women have tales of courage and resilience. Laila had to flee her home in Ghazni during the Taliban years, waiting out the civil war in the Hazara stronghold of Bamian. A round open face, framed by a paisley scarf. Now she has a carpet business in Ghazni with five full-time employees. "The biggest problem," she says, "is security for business owners—and getting long-term loans from banks." She sees a bleak future after the Americans leave: "Obviously, there will be problems for all the people. Life will be hard, especially for women. They have to work hard."

Malalai tells me she is from an open-minded family. After graduating from Kabul University with a science degree, she worked for the UN. When the Taliban took over, they forced women to stay home. "The situation for women was very bad, sitting at home and doing nothing." During the regime, she secretly taught young girls in her house. "I couldn't even carry a pen," she says as her big eyes grow wide. "They would kill me." She's animated, eyebrows dancing, finger-pointing for emphasis as she talks about the Taliban efforts to intimidate her. Now, thanks to a US-funded grant, she has a company that makes silk fabric and scarves. The future? "I am not so optimistic."

Fatima has a slender face and expressive eyes. Educated as a political scientist, she's running an ATM services company that caters to Afghan banks. She has troubles. Wants no questions about her husband or children. After twenty-seven years as a refugee in Iran, she returned to Afghanistan. She started her own company when she "had a problem—I don't like boss." She says, "It's a fact, I am disappointed. After four years in Kabul, I am disappointed."

Noor has a wood business that crafts intricate, hand-carved boxes. She's a Pashtun from Ghazni, elegant in a deep-brown shawl embroidered with turquoise-and-pink arabesques. She looks up to the ceiling as she considers her answers. Her company started in 2001 with just family members, but now over thirty people work in the company. She praises the 10,000 Women project, saying the training helped her organize a business and marketing plan. "I didn't even have e-mail," she says. She is concerned about the recent reduction in USAID grants and loans. On the one hand, she understands that much of the US money was wasted. "They gave it to inexperienced people," she says. On the other, she says she needs the American money to keep going. "I need the capital," she says. She sees "lots of problems" after the Americans leave: "The Taliban will come back and women won't be allowed to work. It will all be repeated."

:   :   :   :   :

USAID is certainly doing its part to keep spreading women's rights money around Afghanistan. In 2012 the agency had announced one of the largest development programs ever: Women in Transition. The enormous program is slated to spend $313 million on women's empowerment programs over the next five years, even though the US troops needed for oversight will be long gone. The ambitious program proposes to place 7,500 Afghan women in government internships, offer business training to women, help Afghan universities develop women's studies programs, and help facilitate networking among accomplished Afghan women. All

laudable on the face of it, but even Afghan female parliamentarian Fark-
hundah Naderi questioned the implementation. "The concept is bril-
liant," she told a *Christian Science Monitor* reporter. "But I hope there is
going to be very strong monitoring. But at the end of the day, effectiveness is so important." And she worried about the destabilizing cultural
effects of eleven years of inordinate amounts of US money being aimed
at women's rights programs that have made little impact, saying, "Men
are jealous."

WIT clearly excites the American director of 10,000 Women in
Afghanistan. She's looking forward to some big contracts. Women in Transition is a veritable feed trough of money—might be $500 million eventu-
ally, she says. She tells me the major beltway bandits are sniffing around
the money. Referencing the powerful, Washington-connected Afghan
women expats, she says, "All the 'Pashtun Princesses' in the US want in."
The director understands the politics. "WIT is one of Secretary Clinton's
legacy projects," she says cannily.

Early in her term as secretary of state, Hillary Clinton lambasted
the waste of US aid to Afghanistan, calling it "heartbreaking." She
cited poor program design, problematic staffing, implementation, and
accountability—the litany of US development failures in Afghanistan.
Despite her promise to increase oversight and monitor "every single dollar" and "track the outcomes," the problems were never fixed.

Yet four years later, as Clinton is leaving office to continue her quest
for the presidency, she is championing the largest USAID program ever
to be funded. It is aimed at Afghanistan, even as the troop levels needed
for oversight are plummeting. Aid to Afghan women continues to poll
well among Democratic women, a major part of Clinton's base.

Policy makers have arrogated and manipulated American women's
appropriate concern about the plight of Afghan women. Time and
again I hear American development officials conflate the brief progressive period in the 1960s, when "women in Kabul went around in mini-
skirts," as the story goes, with the possibilities for women in the hinterlands of Afghanistan, where the deeply conservative customs
continue as they have for centuries. It's like extrapolating the mores of
Manhattan and Malibu to discuss evangelical Alabama and Mormon
Utah.

The ability of a foreign culture to impose its values on another is most often destined to fail, especially if the outsiders are trying to change a thousand-year-old tribal culture buttressed by a powerful and beloved religion. Used to seeing twenty-first-century American storm troopers arriving in primitive Afghan villages to tout women's rights, I began thinking about how Americans would react to eight-foot-high Taliban flying to the United States on armored magic carpets to impose burqas. Bet the rifles would come out, eh?

The lavishly funded women's rights programs have done very little to improve the lives of Afghan women, and even those improvements are likely to be unsustainable. While useful to American politicians pandering to their bases, the contracts are essentially just great fleecing opportunities. As Hillary Clinton knows from experience, most of the WIT money is destined to become "phantom aid," sucked up by development-industrial corporations and well-connected, well-heeled Afghans, albeit some of them women. But very, very little of that money will actually get down to the Afghan women who can use the help. Yes, it is heartbreaking.

: : : : :

Some American women know the reality. The colonel joined the army in the bad days after the Vietnam War. She'd seen the worst of the broken-spirited armed services. Drug and alcohol abuse was rampant. Sexism endemic. But she'd hung in there, rising to become a full-bird colonel. She'd paid her dues, and knew what was what. And she had the soldiers' respect. Remarkably organized, effective, and empathetic, she also had some renown among the young security grunts for her sharp-shooting skills, particularly long-range sniping from a prone position. But the grunts semi-seriously insisted she had a natural advantage: her bosom gave her a more stable shooting platform.

As part of her responsibilities as the deputy commander of a development team in the Pashtun heartland of eastern Afghanistan, she oversaw women's programs. It was an extremely conservative region where women were virtually never seen without burqas, indeed seldom seen at all. In the fundamentalist villages, the American soldiers quickly backpedaled if they happened to encounter a woman, even when she was fully burqa-ed and escorted by a male family member. It was too big a risk. Out on village patrol one day, our Pashtun guide ran ahead to scout for "dogs and women," lest we get into trouble.

I wanted to ask the colonel's help to find an Afghan woman to interview. I was also interested in her views on Afghan gender relations. What had she learned during her rotation? When I asked about interviewing an Afghan woman, maybe the provincial minister of women's affairs, she laughed. "Doug, I've been here for six months, and *I* haven't spoken to an Afghan woman. The minister of women's affairs is gone. She flew to Kabul after her car got bombed." I asked what she thought about the richly funded US efforts to empower Afghan women. She said, "I think that's up to the Afghan women to do."

THIRTY-THREE

Dutch

"STATE DEPARTMENT SAYS AFGHANISTAN ISN'T SAFE," AN understatement if I ever read one. The just-issued State Department advisory set the security threat as "critical." The January 2013 advisory reads, "No region in Afghanistan should be considered immune from violence, and the potential exists throughout the country for hostile acts, either targeted or random, against U.S. and other Western nationals at any time." Stating the obvious, the State Department warning adds, "Afghan authorities have a limited ability to maintain order and ensure the security of Afghan citizens and foreign visitors." The diplomats just noticed?

It's obviously worse than the report indicates: security analysts here in Kabul are saying that every administrative district handed over to Afghan government security forces has actually been handed over to Taliban control. And revolutions begin in the countryside, and then move on to the capital. Kabul's had its worst attacks over the previous two fighting seasons. In September 2011, the insurgents staged a convulsive attack in the heart of Kabul on the US embassy and NATO facilities. The next spring the jihadists launched spectacular coordinated attacks in Kabul that were the largest the capital has suffered in eleven years. Kidnappings are rife. The booms of explosions are so common, people are used to them. Sitting in my little room in besieged Kabul, I keep thinking the insurgents are slowly but surely winning.

I venture out, searching for Afghan-appropriate development that might survive the collapse of the war-inflated Kabubble. The traffic is as chaotic as ever. A hard gray rain is falling. Women in tattered burqas stand beside the crowded roads with their hands out. As my taxi jostles for a lane, I am shocked to see a small girl in sodden clothes kneeling in the street between the rushing cars. Her two hands are raised in supplication. Head up to the falling rain, her open mouth is wide in a cry of anguish.

：　：　：　：　：

The Irishman works for the Dutch Committee for Afghanistan (DCA), a group universally praised for their animal husbandry work, critical in this agriculturally dependent land. He's a balding older development fellow with the soft slouch and compassionate eyes of a kindly professor. He speaks about the DCA's work in a soft brogue. He says, "Our focus is on animal health and reproduction. Period." The group's main mission is to train and support self-sustaining paravets in Afghanistan. "Only in Afghanistan," the Irishman emphasizes, to distinguish the DCA from the avaricious international aid corporations that prowl the underdeveloped world hunting for lucrative contracts.

We're talking in the DCA headquarters, a nondescript compound at the ragged edge of Kabul. The DCA is a small organization, with only about 190 people on staff, the vast majority Afghans, thirty-five of them women. The Irishman is quick to note that he's one of only "two and a half" foreign expats on the DCA staff. "There's me, an Ethiopian, and the 'half' is because one fellow is Pakistani," he smiles.

The DCA has been working in Afghanistan since 1988. "It will be twenty-five years in September 2013," he tells me with obvious pride. DCA runs three paravet training centers, one near Kabul, one in the north near Mazar-e-Sharif and one in the western regions of Herat. "Permissive provinces," he says, distinguishing them from the insurgent-dominated provinces of the south and east.

Determined to provide self-sustaining development, the DCA partnered from the beginning with the local communities. The goal is to train locals, who will return home to be long-term animal health providers in their often subsistence-level farming communities. As a first step, local leaders provide a list of good candidates for DCA paravet training. The DCA then evaluates the nominees. "It's critical to select a proper person," he says.

After vetting, the Afghans are trained for six months at one of the centers. "The curriculum is very basic," he says. The animal husbandry training includes subjects such as vaccinations, immunizations, parasite control, and reproduction. The students also receive business training to help them run a successful practice. "We want to build farmers' knowledge, and improve their economics," he says. "The whole aim is to build a sustainable delivery service at the community level, and deliver a quality service—which is very important."

There are currently 390 DCA-trained paravets working in nineteen of Afghanistan's thirty-four provinces. Both men and women are trained as paravets. "We have a very strong gender program," he says. The DCA respects the tribal proprieties that require male family escorts for women in training. "We work with that. So we've trained brothers and sisters, and husbands and wives. We had one couple who were engaged. They broke up, but both are back in their local community working as paravets."

Once trained, the new paravet receives a basic equipment package, including veterinarian instruments, a signboard, and a refrigerator, crucial to keep vaccines chilled. The refrigerator is often solar powered, as the remote regions seldom have electricity. "In collaboration with the local community, we help the paravet find a suitable location where farmers congregate, places like bazaars and main roads," he explains. The DCA recommends small, affordable clinics—two rooms at most, often in the paravet's home, a far cry from the lavish eight-room vet clinics USAID built across Afghanistan without local input or buy-in. Which, of course, were very soon not used as clinics. "You don't need a great building," the Irishman says. "Their approach is not sustainable."

The DCA model uses a private-sector, fee-for-service framework that is rooted in the subsistence-level Afghan economy, which has a per-capita annual income of about $400. Once the paravet is established, after about six months, the DCA support is technical, not logistical. "We give them an initial input to get them on their feet," he says. Unlike the dominant development model, the DCA-trained paravet is not subsidized long term with international aid money, which predictably dries up when the next politically attractive situation flares. The trained Afghan paravets, called VFUs (Veterinary Field Units), have to pay their own way, including buying supplies—though they do have the advantage of being able to acquire quality DCA medications, which are essential in Afghanistan. "The marketplaces here are full of counterfeit medicines," he says.

"We don't regulate prices," the Irishman says. "That is totally up to the VFU and his clients. This is very pro-poor. Payment is often in barter, like wheat and grain for vet services." The VFUs also organize self-help groups to share information about hygiene, disease, and even business skills. "People crave the knowledge," he says.

The Irishman tells me about the impact: "Paravets definitely are delivering a valuable service to their communities. There's a twenty-five percent reduction in mortality, a twenty-five to thirty percent increase in value. Organizations have done studies, and documented that for every one dollar that's been invested in this program, there is a nine-dollar return on investment. The farmers can see how their animals thrive after deworming, for instance. They come back."

To fund their relatively low-budget programs, the DCA works with a variety of international donors, including UN, Japanese, French, and US organizations. "I'm not going to say anything about USAID. We appreciate their funding," he says after laughing about USAID's obsession with "the burn rate," the bureaucrats' term for spending the entire budget to ensure the same appropriation in the next budget.

Working for so many decades in fractious Afghanistan, the DCA has learned to walk a tightrope between sides that are literally warring. Focused on improving animal health, the DCA preaches political neutrality. From their beginnings during the 1980s Soviet war, and then on through the paroxysm of the 1990s civil war, the DCA worked with Afghan politicians and mujahideen warlords who were battling one another. When the Taliban took power in the 1990s, the DCA encountered new challenges. "It was difficult," he says. "We had to leave for a period—and then came back." After the United States invaded in 2001, the DCA had to cooperate with both the American-led military coalition and the insurgents. And both sides presented difficulties.

Recognizing the DCA's long-term success in Afghanistan, the US military wanted to partner with the Dutch organization. But the military wanted access and information. "You can't have these military show up at vfus," he says. "Or gathering vfus together to ask about their communities. You can't do that." If soldiers showed up at vfus, locals assumed they were allied with the Americans, undermining the trust that paravets had in tribal villages with Taliban loyalties. But despite the NGO community's wariness of the military, the DCA helped some military development teams formulate programs. "I did it," he says with some chagrin. "We did it."

But the US military's short rotations created havoc. Speaking of the military development teams, he says, "They do a fantastic job for six months—and then they leave. Then the new team comes in and starts asking the same questions. It's not productive."

The Taliban also appreciated the DCA-supported paravets. "The Taliban people, they recognized the value of the program. Our mission is to alleviate poverty and food insecurity. We've had our vfus receive letters from the Taliban, permitting them to work. Once some criminals stole a vfu's bike that he used in his work. The Taliban returned it."

"We need to have a neutral business to work in nonpermissive areas," the Irishman tells me. Pointing to a DCA educational poster showing the gestation of a calf through drawings (essential in the generally illiterate hinterlands), he asks, "Do you see any donor logos? No, that's because we have to be neutral to do our work."

"We come again to sustainability," he says in his soft brogue. "It's twenty-five years later, and at times we had no funding, yet it goes on. We can perceive a future without any support, and setting it up to go on." Looking at the poster, he says, "Compared to international donor-supported programs, this is a development policy that lets this private-sector work go on. It's the Afghan way."

THIRTY-FOUR

Intermediates

THE KIDNAPPING NEAR THE FLOWER ST. CAFÉ HAS THE PLACE abuzz. The journalists are tapping away, tweeting the breaking news. Calls from cell phones, working their sources. "French," they say from table to table. Aid worker. Block or two away. Someone shot? Police raiding houses in the neighborhood, but no sign of the kidnappers or the captive. "French pay ransom," one says.

Being Kabul, the Flower St. Café is naturally nowhere near Flower Street. It's in Qale Fatullah, the epicenter of war-zone expatry. With its intense security and California cuisine, the café has been the pivot point for international journalists, NGO consultants, and fellow travelers since an Afghan Californian opened the place in 2003. It's essentially a well-guarded backpacker café for superannuated grad students, many with very high salaries and very big budgets.

I'd come in a little earlier. From my institute to the café, it's only five or six blocks, but it's still a trepidatious walk. The last bit to the café winds down a muddy deserted lane lined with ten-foot-high concrete walls graffitied with advertisements for proposal writing and English lessons. Nervous, I hold my breath when SUVs pass by. There's one of those large graphics I see stenciled all over Kabul that asks in bold black letters, "Cost of War?" Beside a tangle of abandoned razor wire near the café's nondescript entrance, a blue, spray-painted tag announces "Boom Boom Ahmad."

I knock on a narrow metal door set flush into the café's high security walls. A peephole slides open with a sound that says it's steel. An eye glances past me, scanning the street. Once inside the small security chamber, a stony-faced Afghan holds an automatic weapon on me while his partner frisks me and goes through my briefcase. There's a knock on a second steel door, opened by an even harder-faced man with his finger taut on the trigger of a sawed-off pump shotgun. Haunted eyes, wild, matted hair, he has the ravaged look of a killer; the ravaged look of a victim. Afghanistan's been at war for thirty years. The whole country has PTSD.

Once through the security gauntlet, the Flower St. Café is quite lovely. The solicitous staff hurries the food of faraway home to the internationals sitting at the tables. There is an outside garden, where in warm weather diners lounge Afghan-style on shaded *takhts*, wooden platforms with carpets and bolsters. But today it's cold, and people are layered in fleece and down. The Western women are chaste in headscarves. Besides location, security, and Western food, the Flower St. Café has two things going for it: heat and fairly reliable wireless internet. The daily password comes on a small piece of paper.

As I eat my chicken Kiev and spinach salad, European languages surround me: English, French, German, Swedish. The tables and long red banquette are filled with people, most intent on their open laptops, heads bent forward in cyber-benediction. There's a burble of Swedish from the aid workers at next table: "Gambia?" "Ya, Gambia." I overhear them telling the Brits at the next table that Gambia is the next good aid spot. With a pot of green tea, I peck away on an article—good internet and heat are not to be undervalued. It's still hours till Pahlawan fires up the sawdust stove for my evening dose of warmth. I type to the light background music of international travelers' cafés: Gypsy Kings, old dance music, sambas, warbling crooners, vintage jazz, subdued Malian music, noodling African tunes.

And that's when the news of the kidnapping begins to circulate. As people describe where the abduction took place, I think it was very near the bakery where Jebrael warned me about kidnappings. Two tables down someone says the captive is a woman. Someone else says no, that was another kidnapping. Another says the kidnapper was a disgruntled Afghan employee who wanted to grab some of the international money being thrown around. "The French pay ransom," someone repeats. "The French and Italians pay ransom. Not the British. Not the Americans."

Then there's quiet, as we consider how we will get back to our places
safely.

:   :   :   :   :

Meeting over the next days with other journalists covering the war, I
begin to ponder our odd calling. A skittery Afghan combat journalist
who talks, just a little too much, about his handgun and jihadi fighters
in his guesthouse. A tall, lumbering American writer in a stained and
battered baseball cap, returning from an embed with the Afghan army.
A rough embed, he says. People back home are surprised to learn the
Afghan grunts smoke hash before going on patrol. When I mention my
idea of Dorothea Lange–inspired photo portraits of Kabul's war-
damaged security guards, he looks intently at me. Then I ask him about
Kabul's ubiquitous balloon sellers, who blithely tend their airy flocks in
the midst of the ravening traffic, saying the vendors and their wares seem
to be a colorful retort to the grimness of war. Am curious about them.
He looks perplexed, as if he is just remembering the peddlers. "It's good
to have fresh eyes here," he says. "We get too used to this."

One sunny day, I lunch at the café with an Afghan journalist who
strings for the BBC. Quick, assessing eyes set in a broad, open face. Smart
guy, son of a warlord/smuggler who wants him to come home to Kunar
Province and take over the family business. Educated at a New England
liberal arts college, the BBC guy speaks a fast-paced, argot-spiked American English, tempered with an Afghan lilt.

He says the Kabul police chief thinks the kidnapping was an inside
job, a sketchy finance guy. They grabbed a French woman who worked
for an NGO. Another Frenchman got away. Afghan guard shot in the
chest and died. He says the Afghan police were tracking the kidnappers'
cell phones, but their technology only allowed them to vector in to about
fifteen meters, allowing the abductors to get away. Says the French intelligence is furious.

Tells me the US and British governments have strict rules against
paying ransoms to the Afghan kidnappers. Even threaten the captives'
families so they can't pay. "Can't finance terrorism," the diplomats
sniff, even though they sure are doing it through their dysfunctional

development schemes. But many of the European allies quietly pay up, especially the French and Italians. So their citizens get snatched, ransomed, and then go home. American captives just get killed.

We talk about the pressure and exhilaration of war reporting. The grim realities, the taut fears, the unexpected friendships. Thinking about those tense nights flying in vulnerable helicopters, I ask him why the insurgents don't have MANPADS (man-portable air-defense system) like the game-changing Stingers that the CIA gave the mujahideen during the Soviet war. He gives me one of those wise Afghan looks. "Because the US would go after Pakis big time for supplying them to the Taliban," he says with a smile that communicates the duplicity of America and its double-dealing ally. "And secondly," he says, "the CIA still has a big program to buy up old Stingers. There's big advertising billboards at both entrances to Kabul offering to buy up Stingers." He knows none of this makes much sense. It's just the war in Afghanistan.

It's a war that the American public increasingly wants to forget—the shunned war. Even the two presidential candidates essentially ignored the Afghanistan War during their 2012 national convention speeches, though there were still seventy-eight thousand troops on the ground at the time. The war, as they say, polls badly. The US media is following suit with scant coverage. I am speaking with the small remnant band of journalists still covering the Afghanistan War.

Like many journalists I speak with, the BBC guy laments the deadline pressures of today's internet-driven news cycle. "Tweets! They want tweets," he says. "All the time. Breaking news, all the time." And he does his job well, pushing out the nano-news as fast as he gets it. "I feel like a bird in a cage," he says, and asks about independent work.

That night I dream I am working on a factory assembly line. Clean, well-organized place with nice coworkers, easy work, good pay. But I'm miserable, not what I want to do. In the dream I wrestle with wanting to respect my fellow workers while scheming to get out of there. I awake anxious, until I realize I am processing the frustration of journalists stuck with covering the war's undigested "breaking news."

And why do we do it? We want to know something real and unmediated. To see humans in the crucible, and understand our deepest undercurrents. To experience the way that ego vaporizes in the pulsing heat of the moment. Tolerating risk and uncertainty to test ourselves. How did we do?

And there's the adventure. One hot day I am climbing up a steep, rocky wadi with a unit on patrol in the rugged mountains of the Afghan-Pakistani borderlands, a place of a sere and savage beauty. All of us are panting from climbing up the rough track weighed down with our gear. The commander suddenly turns to me and gasps, "You know, back in the states, people pay big bucks for trips like this."

There's always the risk of looking silly. I was talking to a friend just before I left for an Afghanistan embed. He was wondering why soldiers would let a journalist stay with them. I was feeling a little puffed up and said something about how this has been going on since Homer, thinking about his eternal tales of the Trojan War and soldiers' perennial desire for some bard to sing their hero songs. My friend looked puzzled, and then burst out laughing. "Oh, *that* Homer. I was thinking, why would Marge care? I was thinking about Homer Simpson."

For a while that seemed to sum up the importance of war reportage to me—at best some mildly entertaining flail at the truth. If lucky, maybe as telling as *The Simpsons*.

But there are the rewards. At a beer festival I ran into Doc, a medic for a unit I had embedded with during the raging days of the war in 2009. We'd been on some rough missions together in Khost Province. While out in the field, he was phlegmatic, tough. I literally trusted him with my life. I wrote a long essay about his team of soldiers, trying to do the impossible job of development in an active war zone; their tense, scary missions far outside the wire. Doc and his wife had read the article. They'd been at the beer festival a while, and wanted to talk. "I cried," he told me as his wife nodded. "I cried when I read that part about that mission with the IEDs. I didn't know what I was experiencing until I read that. I thought you were writing about somebody else. I heard all that stuff in that village. I knew we were going to get blown up. You were writing about *me*. I was there, but I didn't know about it until I read it."

Much of the reportage of the post-9/11 wars is being done by freelancers, operating without much of a net. It attracts all types. There's the flamboyant Errol Flynns with their Arab *keffiyeh* scarves and loud, arm-waving talk—narcissism and prescription drugs. Quiet guys who listen very, very closely. Intense women journalists bearing down with extraordinary determination and often grace. Shlubby guys, more oblivious than brave, schlepping their gear around for footage and per diems. War-zone tourists, sometimes with curious self-assignments. Reporters who fracture at their fragile points, and need to go home. Hard cases hooked on adrenaline who can't wait for the next hot one. Many seemingly in search of a metatruth that melds the experiences of foreign invaders in a war-torn land with the neo-cosmopolitan, Twitter-addicted lives of Kabul intelligentsia.

The high-paid professional journalists working for old-school established media seem to have more in common with the diplomats and international development consultants than with the impoverished freelancers hanging on with patched-together assignments. One cold night I visit the Kabul correspondent, who works for one of the international dailies. Been reporting from Afghanistan since 2002. His dispatches impress me: he manages to portray the brutal truth of the failing counterinsurgency without alienating his conservative editors.

His invitation for a glass of French wine seems downright debonair after my time on the abstentious military bases. At the cocktail hour, my taxi driver drops me off at a small apartment building near the embassies in the Wazir Akbar Khan neighborhood. The driver idles beside the door until two serious guys with automatic weapons let me in. The correspondent has a very pleasant Western-style apartment, replete with modernist furniture and comfortable sofa configurations. Wine, water, taco chips, pistachios, raisins around the conversation pit. All welcome.

It's a gathering of Kabul's bright young things. His girlfriend, also a journalist, has just moved in from Delhi. There are two lawyers in love sitting side by side on the sofa. The woman works in lawless Afghanistan and Yemen on rule of law issues (that's ROL in development talk). Her new boyfriend is ROL, too. The two scoot a little closer. Ivy League crowd: sharp wits, funny stories, a little one-upmanship. They bond by talking about their houses' fortified safe rooms, one of upscale Kabul's favored real estate amenities, certainly preferable, in my mind, to a sauna or lap pool.

And like kids everywhere, they talk about camp, in this case their hazardous duty training camps that their well-heeled organizations mandated before they left for dangerous postings. At the camps, ex-military guys taught them what to do when attacked or kidnapped. The lawyer jokes that the trainers just want to yell, "You die!" at every scenario. She says, "Ambush training: You die! Anti-kidnapping simulations: You die!" She laughs again, "You can't win." Her boyfriend adds that when he pointed out the pack of young men running through the fancy Sherpur neighborhood carrying rocket launchers, she didn't even notice. "I was concentrating on what we were discussing," she says nonchalantly.

They give me a ride back to the institute, the three of us crammed in the back of the Corolla while up front the driver and guard vigilantly watch Kabul's dark and empty streets. The lawyer says something to them, shakes her head, and speaks again. They nod and turn a corner. She turns to her boyfriend and says, "I keep getting mixed up between Farsi and Arabic. Been doing it all day."

: : : : :

After a quick dinner at the institute, I head out for the nearby Sufi Restaurant. It's on the narrow street where I think the kidnapping happened. I'm curious. Need to know. Heavy snow is slanting down. Even the razor wire is filigreed and laced as Pahlawan opens the gate. One of the Afghan researchers volunteers to go with me, saying it's better if I don't go alone. We chat as we walk down the unlighted lane, his flashlight casting a thin beam. A little uneasy about traipsing down the same street where a kidnapping might have just happened. We enter the warm environs of the restaurant, where the security guard confirms the kidnapping happened yesterday, four doors away. Just wanted to know. Walking back down the lane, I feel something in my jacket pocket. Pulling it out in the dim light, I see it's the tourniquet that the major gave me as a Helmand keepsake. Ah, the souvenirs of Afghanistan.

THIRTY-FIVE

Embassy

THE US EMBASSY IN KABUL IS A FORTRESS-RESORT UNDER construction. There are work crews everywhere on the compound, erecting eight- and ten-story structures. Frantically beeping earthmovers are clawing even more giant holes. It's going to be one of the largest US embassies in the world. The madcap building spree that began in 2009 is proceeding at an almost absurd pace, particularly since the number of Americans in the embassy is plummeting with the military withdrawal. Surveying the thickets of construction cranes, a State Department flack laughingly tells me, "I'm going to hang around. I figure I'll get a whole floor for a penthouse. There won't be anyone here, and look at all this."

Contracted out during the heady days of the surge, the embassy expansion will add a bunch of new buildings to house over twelve hundred additional desks, almost seven hundred more beds, and a posh new recreation center and dining hall. The initial cost was over $625 million. And this is after Obama announced the withdrawal date for American forces, which informs the embassy staffing levels. Even as the embassy numbers are dropping, the State Department keeps beefing up the project. And up goes the price tag. Word had it the embassy expansion is eventually going to cost somewhere upward of three-quarters of a billion dollars—for an embassy in a remote country of about thirty million impoverished people, whose main export is opium, and whose government is, well, shaky. Xanadu in Afghanistan. And, of course, the expansion project is woefully behind schedule, and rumored to be very poorly constructed. "Federal contracts," the flack shrugs.

The flack's a contract public affairs officer. A tall, slender golden boy, he's articulate with that knowing smirk, an Eddie Haskell–like hall monitor mouthing the administration policies with a wink and a nod. We cross the embassy grounds, picking our way past piles of building materials, then descend to the tunnel connecting the two sides of the embassy. The staffers used to just cross the street, but increasing attacks ended open-air perambulations. They became tunnel people a long time ago and aren't coming up anytime soon. So much for "We are winning the war." There has been a change since I was last there: the concrete tunnel walls are now covered with enormous photo murals of scenic America, comforting pictures of mountains and seashores and fields of waving grain. Ignore that man in the turban with the Kalashnikov. You are not in a tunnel in Afghanistan, you are really in HolidayLand America.

Heading down the hall to the embassy dining room, the flack points to an elaborate architect's rendering of the finished complex. "Take a look at that," he smiles. The colorful rendering promises the new embassy compound will be complete "by 2014." Drawn in the hopeful early days of Obama's surge, the drawing shows a charming campus-like embassy, with the road reopened and nary a security wall to be seen. There's a turnaround that curls directly in front of the embassy front door, to allow visitors to hop out just right there. A green soccer field for cavorting Kabulis perks up the design. No razor wire; no blast barriers; no rings of intense security. Won't life be lovely in this imagined halcyon future?

The reality: One evening after meeting with USAID officials, I am walking through the embassy grounds toward the main security gate near Massoud Circle. Razor-wired fences and blast barriers and checkpoints with armed guards punctuate the quarter-mile or so walk. Halfway to the gate, I suddenly encounter an historic vestige of the US embassy security from a far more hopeful time. It's a large blue-bordered sign that's hand-lettered in faded red-and-black paint. It reads in English and Dari, "The US embassy would be grateful if any of our friends who have information on terrorist activity or threat information to please come to this gate." It strikes me with a chill that Afghans used to be able to walk to this point in the compound, now deeply buried behind concentric rings of hard security. So that's how it's really gone in the dozen years since the United States invaded Afghanistan.

:   :   :   :   :

The State Department is clearly conflicted about my presence. When I arrived back at the Kabul airport a few days before, a sergeant handed me an e-mail from a State Department public relations officer, inviting me to take part in an embassy roundtable discussion about the war. About the same time, a staffer for John Sopko, the Special Inspector General for Afghanistan Reconstruction, e-mailed that Sopko was in Kabul and wanted to meet. For security reasons, he tells me, we'll need to meet in the embassy. In 2008 the US Congress established SIGAR to be a watchdog over the taxpayer money flooding into Afghanistan. A former federal narcotics prosecutor, Sopko knows malfeasance when he sees it. Sopko and his team have accordingly been aggressive in their investigations and disclosures. They are blowing the whistle on the scandalous US reconstruction fiasco as loud as they can, to the discomfort of the military, State Department, and USAID. Given the drawdown and the widespread reconstruction scandals in Afghanistan, SIGAR is urging Congress to strategically reconsider further aid appropriations, to perhaps "postpone, reduce, cancel, reinforce, redesign or repurpose projects." So I am particularly looking forward to conferring with Inspector General Sopko.

Well, neither meeting happens. When I ask the flack about the roundtable, he gives me that insider grin and clams up. Then I begin to get frustrated e-mails from the SIGAR staffer. The State Department at the embassy won't let this independent, congressionally mandated inspector general meet with me unless we include a striped-pants chaperone. The staffer calls, says Sopko is furious, demanding a private meeting without handlers, rampaging around the embassy—stay tuned. But the diplomats won't budge. No talking unless the monitor is present. Pretty funny. Do they think we are going to pass notes? The staffer finally e-mails that Sopko and I will just have to meet in Washington.

It is not the only challenge. The military put the SIGAR investigators on a tight leash, refusing to provide security to areas outside of a one-hour round trip from an advanced medical facility, claiming they want to provide "adequate security and rapid emergency medical support." Right. Though military and development money is still pumping into Afghanistan with minimal oversight, the withdrawal of essential military security restricts SIGAR investigators to one-fifth of the country.

Some time later, I talk to a State Department foreign affairs officer about the Sopko meeting the diplomats scotched. "Well," she sniffs, "it is our embassy." "Really," I say, "I thought it was *our* embassy." We agree to disagree. Later talking about the aid appropriation bonanza, she snarkily admits, "We were embarrassed about how much money was being wasted . . . but with the military doing development?" While there is plenty of blame to go around for the botched development, her snippy comment reminds me of the general who said, "Defense is from Mars, State is from Venus."

I am more taken aback with the realization that only a few generations ago, the American military won two wars, and American diplomats and technocrats reconstructed devastated Europe and Japan. In the process, they kept Western Europe democratic, and democratized Japan to boot, a country that considered its emperor a deity. Now the military can't even win a war against a ragtag insurgency, and our best and brightest are too busy punching their tickets to notice they can't even reform a country whose tribally based trading culture makes them ideal candidates for back-scratching democratic politics.

The flack and I have lunch in the embassy dining facility. Same steam-tabled contractor food that I ate out in the forward operating bases. Same hothouse high school cafeteria feel, with claques and cliques huddled together at the tables. As we eat our canned and defrosted fare off the pasteboard plates, we politely parry, me the persistently inquiring journalist, he the bemused professional public relations officer.

Traveling around the war zones, I realized "counterinsurgency" had become an off-limits word among the military. It's now the embarrassingly failed strategy, though no one wants to openly admit it. Did the denial extend to the State Department? I coyly ask the flack when the embassy had given up on counterinsurgency (COIN in the argot). "Off the record," he says reflexively. "A year or so ago, when Karzai kept smacking us, criticizing the US for everything, there was kind of a collective shrug here in the embassy. COIN was over. Fuck him."

The flack gives me the party line with an arched eyebrow: how well things are going; the increasing strength of the Afghan security forces; the peace initiatives with the Taliban; the new ambassador's effectiveness—yada yada.

Of course, all of this is just spin. The Taliban-led insurgency is controlling more and more ground in the countryside and Kabul is racked with insecurity. The jihadis have no need to make peace. They are winning. The US-Afghan alliance is troubled, to say the least. President Karzai had been whaling away at the United States for quite a while. Recently threatened to join the Taliban, now blames the endemic corruption on the Americans. One day at the embassy I run into the British embassy's head PR person, who is going to meet with her American counterpart. When I joke that they are probably meeting to plan world domination or something of the sort, she breezily rejoins, "It's all about manipulation and perception, manipulation and perception."

THIRTY-SIX

LOSS

ANNE SMEDINGHOFF IS DIPLOMATIC, EXPLAINING I CAN'T bring my recorder to the embassy meeting with the threat finance guy. Security, you know. But no worries, she says, she'll be there with her recorder. She holds up her tiny little machine. She'll send me an MP3 of the interview, no problem. I'd been in the embassy before with my recorder, but whatever.

Anne Smedinghoff is a rising twenty-five-year-old diplomat, an assistant information officer. She's my minder, assigned to escort me to an interview with a Justice Department official who is heading up the Afghan Threat Finance Cell (ATFC). The cell is charged with finding and disrupting sources of Taliban funding, particularly the hundreds of millions in US military and development money that the insurgents and their corrupt Afghan government enablers have skimmed. I'd interviewed members of the multiagency cell in the past, reporting on their work. When I contacted the threat finance guy, he was happy to speak with me about the cell's current work. The State Department less so. Took some wrangling, but finally got an embassy interview scheduled. Security, you know.

In many ways, Smedinghoff is representative of many young American women working in Afghanistan, where they can combine adventure with a career-enhancing posting and hefty paychecks plumped with danger pay. For Smedinghoff, the manipulation and perception job is part of the assignment.

As we walk to the meeting room, Smedinghoff quizzes me about life outside the embassy compound, as the staff is trapped inside. When I mention some of the Kabul restaurants, she tells me the State Department banned dining at most places outside the embassy. She longs for a good pizza. I ask about her path from her home in the Chicago suburbs to this Kabul powder keg. Catholic high school, Johns Hopkins international studies, then the State Department. An interesting post in Venezuela. Then on to Afghanistan. Anne Smedinghoff is lively, bright, educated, and funny; poised and gracious in a natural way. Brimming with youthful vitality, accomplishments, and promise, she is the daughter any parent would be proud to have.

We talk about my embeds in Zabul and Helmand, and she tells me that in Venezuela she could explore the hinterlands when not working. But here in Afghanistan, she's penned up like most foreign service officers. She tells me she wants to "break the wire" in the worst way. "On a good day, this is like a small liberal arts college," she laughs. "On a bad day it's like a maximum security prison."

:   :   :   :   :

The meeting with the threat finance guy goes very well. He has a lot to tell me, talking in agitated bursts about the challenges to keep US and opium money out of the Taliban's hands. He's an intense, buttoned-down guy who's clearly frustrated by the way things are going. He laments the ATFC's meager funding of $400,000 a year and the sparse staffing, which has been cut from sixty-seven to fifty-three despite their important mission. But the cell has been effective anyway. "Because we were born poor," he says, "we've stayed frugal."

The threat finance guy talks about the ATFC role in cracking open the Kabul Bank scandal, an almost $900 million Ponzi scheme of fraudulent loans that led up into the highest levels of the Afghan government. A cynical USAID financial officer earlier told me that given the amount of money the United States was pushing on the Afghan insiders who were "bankers," he didn't blame them for stealing it. After the exposé, the United States and its allies had to prop up the Afghan government budget to cover the losses that represented 5 percent of Afghanistan's annual economic output. "It was not only a Ponzi scheme," the threat

finance guy says, "it was also a money-laundering operation," with ties
to the insurgents. He notes that Afghan movers and shakers have "very
little incentive" to crack down on corruption. Even when Afghan politicians are indicted for major corruption, they seldom get more than
"smacked on the wrist."

He estimates that 50 percent of the Taliban funding is skimmed from
US military logistics and development contracts, as well as payoffs from
US-funded cell phone companies, banks, utilities, and other Afghan
private enterprises. Most of the rest comes from the US-condoned opium
trade.

I scribble, trying to keep up with his torrent of information and in-
vective, but don't worry too much, because both Smedinghoff and the
ATFC's State Department liaison have their recorders out. Lying right
there on the table, while the two women assiduously take their own
notes. I can always refer to that MP3 recording she promised. But I never
get that recording, despite a number of e-mails to Smedinghoff. Just
doing her job, I guess.

Smedinghoff's career continued to go well after I left Kabul. She was
a comer. Her colleagues started calling her Ambassador Anne. When
Secretary of State John Kerry arrived in Kabul in late March for an official visit, the embassy assigned Smedinghoff the plum job of escorting
him. She was his control officer. As she did with other people, she made
an impression on her big boss.

Anne Smedinghoff did eventually get to break the wire—and in the
worst way. A few weeks after the successful Kerry visit, she escorted a
group of Afghan journalists on a media day down to Qalat City, the
capital of Zabul, the Taliban-controlled province that so interested her
when we met. It was one of those winning-hearts-and-minds missions,
in this case to distribute schoolbooks that the US corporation Scholastic
had donated to My Afghan Library, an aid program jointly run by the
State Department and the Afghan Ministry of Education. Scholastic
wanted some good press for their donation. An e-mail from the embassy
public relations office stated, "Scholastic would like to see more media
reporting." So the mission was a WHAM photo op to get some press for
an American corporation while pretending Zabul was secure and still

receiving US aid. "A media extravaganza," a military briefing called it. "Happy snaps," the security grunts derisively termed these PR events that they hated to guard.

In my experience there, Qalat City was a wild and woolly, ambush-prone place, where the military units took extraordinary security precautions before venturing from the tightly guarded US compounds. To travel two miles across Qalat City, we had to drive in a convoy of five armored MRAPs accompanied by a heavily armed security platoon.

So I was stunned to later learn that Anne Smedinghoff and a group of journalists were walking around Qalat City—lost. That seemed insane. Taliban suicide bombers detonated their explosives near them, killing her and four other Americans, including three soldiers and an interpreter. Other Americans were grievously wounded. It was an egregious breakdown in operational security. An army report stated that the mission "was plagued by poor planning that failed at all levels." And it was a great loss.

I exchanged e-mails of condolences with the embassy public relations officer, who was a great friend of hers. I saw heart-wrenching tributes to Anne Smedinghoff posted online. Secretary Kerry eulogized her, praising her idealistic commitment to "changing people's lives." He noted the "extraordinary harsh contradiction" of her being killed while carrying books to a school. He described the Zabul media event as "a confrontation with modernity," and said Smedinghoff embodied "everything that our country stands for." It did little to salve my dismay that yet another promising American had been lost for such a dubious, failed cause. I thought of the remarks Kerry made on Capitol Hill in 1971, when he was a young, antiwar Vietnam vet. The then twenty-seven-year-old Kerry poignantly asked America, "How do you ask a man to be the last man to die in Vietnam? How do you ask a man to be the last man to die for a mistake?"

THIRTY-SEVEN

Optimism

WHAT WILL BE AFGHANISTAN'S FUTURE AFTER THE AMERICANS leave? I ask the Afghan government official. How does he feel about things? How will it go when the Americans are gone? He's a natty finance analyst in a tailored sport coat, turtleneck, and suede Hush Puppies. Trimmed beard; short hair; toothy smile in a slender face. Educated and articulate, he is part of the expatriate class that thundered back to Afghanistan after the American invasion to take up the reins of power and privilege. A perky technocrat with a head for numbers, he could land on his feet in an earthquake. I ask again, what is the future for Afghans after the American withdrawal? He smiles and says brightly, "I am hopeless—but optimistic."

We sit in his gloomy government office inside one of the guarded American compounds near the embassy. It's a cold, gray day. He tells me the five-story Afghan government building used to be a Taliban prison. He points out the window to a low brick structure standing just outside, and says it's a kindergarten the CIA built for Afghan officials' children. "CIA just down there," he nods toward another nearby building. I am befuddled. Why would the CIA build a kindergarten? He shrugs and says smoothly, "As an Afghan, I really appreciate the American efforts."

"The country has been changed," the technocrat says. "I'm a person who works in statistics," he says. "I count things. Things have changed. To build an army, a police force, an intelligence agency in ten years is an accomplishment. They are completely blind, the people who think it's a lost cause." A process guy, he praises the Afghan government's recent "budget execution," the standard fiscal planning that is one of the great goals of the American "nation-building" campaign. Getting Afghan ministries and provincial governments on budgets seemed to be the be-all and end-all of counterinsurgency for a while, sending hundreds of armed convoys of WHAM warriors out on Business 101 missions with bored Afghan officials. As best I could see, the officials didn't want to know how to account for US largesse. They just want to know how much money they could have to steal.

In a way, the technocrat's continuing presence in Kabul is laudable. Many have already fled. Applications for refugee visas are skyrocketing. Afghan diplomats are taking advantage of the opportunity and just not returning when their postings are up. One American analyst dealing with corruption told me graft actually got worse after the surge started because the corrupt Afghans had more to grab, and the relatively honest ones figured they'd better get some so they would have money to leave.

Parroting the standard Afghan officials' line, the technocrat tells me the United States needs to keep a military presence in Afghanistan—six to ten thousand troops indefinitely, he thinks. "If you withdraw," he says, leaning forward, "there will be a psychological impact on the Taliban and the government. This is a very bad idea. It's vital for the region that the US stays." He cites rising pan-Islamic movements in Iran and Pakistan, as well as China's increased interest in central Asia. "China has its own economic agenda here," he says.

He claims the Afghan security forces are succeeding against the Taliban. "There is only one problem," he says. "The leadership of the Afghan security forces is lacking. It's been replaced by criminals, drug lords, warlords." He laments the corruption and power grabs surrounding the upcoming presidential election as the old tribal warlords jockey for spoils. "They are trying to flex themselves," he says. "These people are playing a divisive game." He laughs about the chances of an honest election, explaining the government officials have already distributed over three times as many voting cards, which permit voting on election day, as there are eligible Afghan voters.

He tells me a naughty secret: The Americans are willing to pay so much for gasoline to run their war machine that clever Afghan insiders smuggle embargoed Iranian petrol over the border to western Afghanistan, where they store the cheap fuel in underground storage tanks before selling it to the US military at wildly inflated prices—hundreds of bucks a gallon, I'd heard. "The political elite," he says, "they are just criminal networks."

:   :   :   :   :

I taxi through the slush to another interview. Passing through the Sherpur neighborhood that is crowded with grotesque new mansions, my driver points to a huge, multistory marble palace beribboned with razor wire and studded with security cameras. "That's General Dostum's," he says, naming the powerful Uzbek warlord/government official. The driver says Dostum owns five houses in Sherpur, the neighborhood that became infamous after President Karzai and his cohorts stole the land from poor residents soon after taking power. The driver mordantly says the neighborhood nickname is something like "Cha-pur," which means "capturing land." With the drawdown, the air is quickly going out of the Sherpur bubble. USAID used to rent one eighteen-room honker for $24,000 a month. The price has dropped to less than half. And the leases are now very, very short term.

We head to a newish office building tucked behind the Soviet-era Russian Cultural Center. I'm interviewing an elegantly be-suited government minister, whose sleek office is tricked out with the accoutrements of Afghan power: an immense, intricately woven carpet overlaid with even finer carpets, a sprawling wooden desk gleaming with polish, and a long, black leather sofa. He's in charge of bankrupt Afghan banks—obviously an important job with a long future.

The minister is another expatriate who came home after the American occupation. Born in Nangahar Province near the Khyber Pass, he grew up as a refugee in Pakistan, where his devout Muslim family fled after the Russians invaded in the 1980s. He began his education in Islamic madrassas, and then graduated from an Islamic university. "As a child," he says, "I wanted to be a scholar. I had a natural inclination to be a philosopher." His grizzled beard, thick eyebrows, and intense eyes give him the gravitas of a wise, learned mullah. During the years when the Taliban held power, he earned a law degree from a Texas university, passing up a chance to stay in the United States to return to Afghanistan in

2007. "It's been a life full of surprises," he says. "This was my aim from day one. It was to return. You love the place where you are born."

Like many returning Afghans, he came with great dreams. "There was expectation and hope. It would be a new Afghanistan, democratic and peaceful. But unfortunately we are far from our goals. It's heartbreaking, this destruction. Disappointments, challenges are to be expected, but we were unable to establish and institute a rule of law. We didn't implement our own laws."

He talks about the international community's failure to understand Afghanistan's society: "This is a very tough country," he says about the independent, bellicose Afghans. "They love their religion. They don't like change." And he complains about the US-led coalition's failure to insist that the new Afghan government operate honestly: "The international community was in no hurry. There were no systems; no laws. These things made the journey tougher and tougher."

So a tribal society without a tradition of formal secular law became a country of Western-financed corruption and violence. Billions of dollars of international aid was stolen and wasted, with little development to show for it. He says, "There were two improvements: roads and schools—but sustainability? If only they had just divided all that money among the people. This was the golden opportunity for Afghanistan—and it was lost," he says with a sigh.

I ask him the same question I'd asked other Afghans: What will happen to Afghanistan after the Americans are gone? He looks at me for a few moments with assessing eyes, and then wryly says, "As an Afghan, I have to be optimistic. I have no other choice."

Epilogue

SO I FLEW HOME TO AMERICA, MY CURIOSITY SATISFIED. I knew how the story ended. The news I had to share: nothing had changed. The same toxic system that connected ambitious American careerists, greedy US military and development corporations, Afghan kleptocrats, and their jihadi collaborators was alive and well in Afghanistan. A sardonic intelligence officer had told me years before, "It's the perfect war. Everyone is making money." And that was still the case. Nothing had changed. Time and again while traveling across devolving Afghanistan, I asked officers and officials that classic military after-action question: What were the lessons learned? And all I got were blank stares.

Soldiers on the ground knew the hearts-and-minds counterinsurgency strategy was a strategic disaster. "The Afghans ain't buying what we're selling," one Skol-dipping sergeant said after yet another attack on his development team. I heard grunts say again and again, "The juice ain't worth the squeeze." A shrewd colonel told me, "I don't think the American public expects us to be efficient—the fog of war, the friction of battle, all that. But they do, however, expect us to be *effective*."

The scorecard on America's fourteen years (and counting) of war in Afghanistan: A trillion dollars has been wasted and tens of thousands of American and Afghan lives have been ruined, but the Afghan government remains one of the world's most corrupt and dysfunctional. After receiving more development aid than any country in history, Afghanistan's impoverished society is still at the bottom of almost every development index. And after confronting the world's greatest military power, the Taliban-led insurgency controls most of the countryside and increasingly imperils Kabul and other major cities. A tale of hubris, ignorance, farce, and greed. And failure.

The post-9/11 Afghan government was a failed state from the beginning, little more than a corrupt satrapy of US-allied drug lords and tribal power mongers, operating behind a thin scrim of sham elections. The unitary constitution that the US-led international powers imposed on the historically tribalized Afghans after the invasion did little but centralize graft. The pattern continued with the US-engineered "unity government" of rivals Ashraf Ghani and Abdullah Abdullah. In the chaos after the fraudulent 2014 presidential election, Secretary of State John Kerry jiggered the joint governance deal to fend off impending civil war. His pitch to the two camps: figure it out and share the loot. Don't collapse on the Obama watch.

The laughingly misnamed "unity government" was at best a temporary fix. A year after the Ghani-Abdullah administration took office, they still couldn't agree on a secretary of defense, and the Afghan security forces were more notable for corruption and ghost soldiers than effectiveness. The insurgency's increasing strength during the 2015 fighting season was evident. The near-collapse of Afghan government forces in the fight for the important provincial city of Kunduz prompted Obama to break his promise to withdraw US troops from Afghanistan. He kicked the can into the next administration. America's endless war in Afghanistan.

:   :   :   :   :

After decades of war, Afghanistan and America are both suffering national cases of PTSD, with the historical price yet to be determined. War-ravaged Afghanistan is tragically hurtling toward another massive humanitarian crisis. America is suffering from its post–Cold War failure of leadership, which has facilitated the power of the self-serving Deep State. War has been good for the 1%ers. And the same powerful American forces that have benefited so mightily from the two failed post-9/11 wars are intent on taking the same discredited show on the road to other intractable regions of the Middle East and Africa. Afghanistan and Iraq were great gigs for them. Why stop now?

There are many victims in this story, War on Terror veterans among them. As the US military rapidly downsizes, long-serving veterans with multiple post-9/11 rotations are being cut loose. Veteran services are increasingly underfunded and overwhelmed. Realizing their patriotism was appropriated and their service is now undervalued, many soldiers are angry.

But as with war eternal, the venal and the noble are inseparably annealed. Coursing across Afghanistan, I encountered time and again the selflessness, determination, and courage that define the best of what it means to be human. I saw men and women, American and Afghan alike, transformed and elevated by duty and love of their compatriots. I saw the remarkable strength and resilience of the Afghan people, along with their exceptional intelligence and wit; their artistry and love of beauty; their deep devotion to their religion, their families, and their country. I met American after American determined to make the world a better place, in part by reforming the United States' role in it.

Index

DOUGLAS A. WISSING is an award-winning journalist and author of eight books, including *Funding the Enemy: How US Taxpayers Bankroll the Taliban* and *Pioneer in Tibet: The Life and Perils of Dr. Albert Shelton*. He has contributed to the *New York Times, Washington Post, Los Angeles Times, Foreign Policy*, Asia Times, Salon.com, GlobalPost, CNN, and BBC, among other media outlets.